A CIVILISED BEGINNING

(the Human Social Journey)

Hamid Soltani

ISBN: 978-1-925515-09-1
Published by Vivid Publishing
P.O. Box 948, Fremantle
Western Australia 6959
www.vividpublishing.com.au

Cataloguing-in-Publication data is available from the National Library of Australia

Book cover image by Simon King
Cover design by Amir Aligorgi

The Human Social Journey

This is a book about the journey of human awakening and is dedicated to humanity. It describes what is glaringly wrong with our current crumbling civilisation, what the root causes of our social failings are, how to prepare and reinvent ourselves as a free race for a better civilised world of existence. Finally it offers ways to go about achieving a sustainable, harmonious existence.

The Author

Hamid Soltani is the founder of Soltani Therapy. His main professional focus encompasses topics such as the human and social consciousness, systems dynamics, human intelligence, psychosomatics and psychotherapy. Hamid is a practicing life coach, clinical hypnotherapist and a management consultant in cultural change and transformation.

Hamid has pioneered a set of perspectives and body of knowledge on the concept of 'what and who we are' and 'why and how' we interact with life the way we do. His work is also about our experiences in life and how we are privileged to consciously change them as we please to create different experiences and realities. This work is called Soltani Therapy.

Hamid holds a fundamental view that most things in life are possible as long as we can first imagine them. His work is about the art of authentic knowing and he welcomes the opportunity to share his findings with audiences as far and as wide as possible.

Resist digesting lies

When it comes to controlling human beings there is no better instrument than lies. Because, you see, humans live by beliefs and beliefs can be manipulated. The power to manipulate beliefs is the only thing that counts.

—**Michael Ende**

The truth is messy. It's raw and uncomfortable. You can't blame people for preferring lies.

—**Holly Black**

There is beauty in truth, even if it's painful. Those who lie, twist life so that it looks tasty to the lazy, brilliant to the ignorant, and powerful to the weak. But lies only strengthen our defects. They don't teach anything, help anything, fix anything or cure anything. Nor do they develop one's character, one's mind, one's heart or one's soul.

—**José N. Harris**

Your dignity can be mocked, abused, compromised, toyed with, lowered and even badmouthed, but it can never be taken from you. You have the power today to reset your boundaries, restore your image, start fresh with renewed values and rebuild what has happened to you in the past.

—**Shannon L. Alder**

The worst part about being lied to is knowing you weren't worth the truth.

—**Jean-Paul Sartre**

Acknowledgement

To my beautiful wife Jan, who I depended heavily on while I was writing this book. She is the dearest thing in my life and her presence makes my life shine ever so brightly.

My beautiful late mother Sarvenaz who was my deep inspiration in life. Her love and compassion for humanity strongly influenced me in my general outlook on life, prepared me for my clinical work to help others and in my publications. I owe her immensely with every ounce of my being.

My larger family members who constantly challenge the status quo and always are preoccupied with the esoteric side of life for the sake of greater knowing and social contribution.

My dear friends who are always there to hear my points of view with care, patience and wise introjection.

My sweet and patient dog Zeus who played a major role in maintaining my sanity by periodically dragging me away from writing to play ball with him. Thank you my beautiful dog.

My challenges as a writer

The hardest challenge for me when I first thought of writing this book was how I should go about structuring my accumulated thoughts, knowledge and wisdom in order to successfully reach my readers with my intended messages. I also had to think about how I should give my audience real value and do it without either scaring them off with too much information and facts or losing them altogether in the unintended gaps as my story unravel? The following summary points highlight some of the challenges and solutions I had to apply while I was writing this book.

The concepts discussed in this book relate to life complexities, esoteric and abstract nature of reality – the forces that shape us that we are all subjected to, the ones that bring our joys and struggles in our daily lives. The question for me was how I should effectively sequence these intriguing concepts and make them easy to grasp and palatable to my deserving readers. Knowing that too much science can be blinding and too little substantiation of the presented facts on the other hand, can also take away from the credibility of the story and do injustice to its findings. I chose the middle ground and diligently tried to stay focused, logical and tell my story as simply as I can to those who are ready and wish to hear it.

My ideas and the topics in this book have been evolving over many years of my hunger, dedication and search for meaningful questions & answers to life and the universe and also by:

- witnessing, understanding and addressing a diverse range of clients with life and psychological needs;

- clinical research and trials;

- working as a management consultant to organisations;

- exploring a variety of concepts such as the Human and Social Psychology, Systems Sciences including Cybernetics, Quantum Physics and Ancient Spiritual Perspectives & Wisdoms, and most importantly;

- the application of basic common sense to problem solving.

As the true nature of reality is highly speculative, and with each ideological camp tightly subscribing to its own subjective definitions of what reality is, it often represents yet another interesting challenge for a genuine writer who wishes to effectively communicate his or her stories to a diverse mix and wide ranging audience. Can a human idea with one set of definitions and meanings attract and interest others holding a different set of meanings and definitions for the same idea? How can a person communicate to another person who embraces contrasting views, beliefs and interpretations of the topic in question? The solution I applied to this challenge was to allow my sense of sincerity, authenticity and integrity of my art to permeate and speak in my general writing. I allowed factors such as inclusivity of a diverse range of views and respect of all ideologies for what they represent.

I believe there is a common unspoken language accessible to all who wish to consciously tune to it. It is found when you are centred and deeply aligned. In spite of different individual ideologies, people at this frequency somehow get deeply connected to one another and lose themselves in an undifferentiating sea of oneness, call it 'trust' if you wish. This language allows their fears and persistent resistance to new perspectives to subside and openness for new experiences and possibilities to flourish.

This language is the expression of our authentic love and passion for life, its mystery and the unravelling of imagined future experiences. It allows us to realise and experience great and inspiring qualities both in ourselves and others.

The aim of this book is to reveal to curious readers, what life means from a wider perspective of the systemic universe and how we may come to the realisation that out of all potential options and choices, we are able to consciously choose the most relevant, inspiring and empowering possibilities for ourselves in life. In order to achieve such objectives in writing this book, to the best of my ability, I have included concepts that are as truthful and validated by a number of scientific & social communities and somehow elegantly lined up with the main theme of ancient wisdom and practices.

My main purpose in life is to reach out and help people who want to be helped with what I know and am capable of delivering. This book is an example of this and my intention is to help and make a difference to those people I can reach. While we are on the subject of helping, I need to mention, this also created another challenge for me how I should provide help to another person and in what situation the help can effectively be received by the recipient. For me to address this, I also had to first question 'who needs help, who wants help and how help can be given.

We often hear or come across people who appear to be in need of help. They could be physically or mentally in trouble or pain. Some may ask for help and others keep their sufferings to themselves. People who are experiencing traumas often have some definitive views or clarity in their minds about:

- what their actual problems are (their perceived views);

- what type of solution would be appropriate for them, and

- how and in what way the solution may work for them.

The problem here is – 1) the actual diagnosis of the nature of human problems, and 2) the subsequent application of real solutions can be highly challenging for the following reasons.

How does anyone know the exact nature of their current pains or problems? How does anyone distinguish between the symptoms and the actual root causes? If we don't know the exact nature of our problem, our corresponding solution to our misdiagnosed problem becomes a futile exercise.

To know the real issues causing individual sufferings is the first important step towards the end-to-end process of successful self-healing. Without an accurate identification of the root causes, at best, we can only tamper with things we don't clearly understand and at worst, we can do an untold amount of damage. As previously mentioned, the sufferers often project in their minds what they perceive causing their issues. Therefore in the majority of cases, the sufferer's subjective perspective on the exact nature of their problems could be the first serious hurdle towards an effective healing process.

Who Needs Help?

In accordance with our common caring human nature, I am sure you agree that whoever is having a bad experience or is suffering should immediately qualify for help and be given help in the best possible way. This concept is a given and not in question here. However, the potential problem arises when a person in need of help, places terms and conditions on how they may receive help and in what quantities, especially when they may not have enough wisdom to make sense of the problem and solution in the first place. Through their subjective biases, they may deny alternative views. The person with such an approach often eliminates new potentials and fruitful possibilities in their lives. This behaviour occurs mainly due to their deeper fixations and subsequent rejections of any proposed alternative solutions to their problems

Therefore, based on the Cybernetics Ashby's law of Requisite Variety, there were two options available to me for pleasing my audience, I could either:

- become selective in the type of audience I would like to please and specialise in certain demographics and people with potentially higher levels of readiness, aptitude and hunger for personal growth or;
- develop materials to allow for a more diverse range of personal readiness in the content of my book.

So I decided to focus my writing on readers with greater personal interest and burning passion for discovering their essence of being and their position within this great mystery called life. In all sincerity, you – the deserving reader – would enjoy this book if your level of current perspectives and beliefs are somewhat aligned to the main thrust of this book. For those of you I may have failed to reach, deeply touch or have disappointed in any way, please accept my apology.

Finally, even though I enjoy documenting my views and concepts, I admit that I am not an artful literary writer, perhaps you should think of me as a story teller with a passion to share his accumulated perspectives with others. In my view; in the end, the message is what matters and those who are meant to see and understand them will do so at this point in time.

Hamid Soltani

Table of Contents

1.

Introduction

Whichever way we may look, we can't escape from the fact that there are some fundamental and glaring flaws in how we collectively live in this world. We instinctively and intelligently know that what we socially witness somehow doesn't add up or make direct sense to how we expect it to be.

Most of the population of the world (all mums and dads in this world) innately and naturally would love to live and raise their children in an inspiring and nurturing world of unity and yet, somehow they find themselves living in a divided world of chaos, suffering and turmoil. WHY?

We generally dislike and don't regard human cruelties as the plausible civilised option as we diligently try hard to avoid such nastiness as best as we can. Yet, somehow we live in a world that it is quite normal and totally legitimate for a large scale worldwide arms industry to officially exist and to legally flourish with no limits, generating trillions of dollars for a handful of people in the world. On a daily basis, we shudder in horror as we witness how such hideous destructive arms are routinely used in barbaric wars everywhere around the world. How can such brutal contradiction continue to exist in our world?

We generally would like to experience personal freedom and expect our human values and rights to be respected by others. Yet collectively and internationally we witness our human rights and values to be systemically abused and compromised often by our own officials. How is this possible and why is it socially tolerated?

We are benevolent at heart and do not like to see massive disparity between have and have not, yet a small minority in this world are allowed to enjoy the majority of the generated wealth while many are starved and homeless. Why does our official system allow such inequalities to exist?

We may not admit openly, but deeply we all somehow feel connected to nature and respect our prized mother earth. We instinctively appreciate the preciousness and finite significance of our natural resources, yet on a daily basis we witness our fragile environment to be systemically ignored and ruthlessly destroyed simply for greed and no social advancement for our humanity. If it is not the masses, then who endorses and gives the green light for the systemic vandalism and destruction of our precious planet Earth?

Deep down we don't quite understand why humanity has been so systemically deprived and not given the opportunity to live in a cleverly designed civilised world? Our global social designers have had plenty of opportunities through thousands of years of human evolution and easy access to the greatest scientific solutions available, They could intentionally and competently design, develop and deliver a civilised social structure that all of us can enjoy and prosper. Yet, our organised governing bodies have mysteriously failed to deliver such a civilised social platform. They somehow find it easier to land a space craft on a moving asteroid or develop amazingly complex weaponry than create a cohesive and functioning social world for their citizens. WHY?

Just remember the above mentioned failed global practices and injustices have existed for the entire history of humanity and are not just recent emerging phenomena. In equal proportion and intensity, so do the cries of innocent people throughout the world for justice and fairness also go back throughout our entire human history .The overall result of our social make up and the systemic structure has resulted in massive social, political and environmental crises.

The experiences of recent years have brought us closer to become more concerned about the future health of our global social system. Our young people by and large don't trust official establishments anymore and are generally disillusioned about their future opportunities for jobs, housing and welfare. Our senior citizens are nervous with the current state of global financial institutions and question their prospects of living in a world of peace and stability. The glaring gap between rich and poor has increased exponentially. The threat of barbaric wars across the globe has become our nightmarish reality and our social and economic concerns for refugees and globally displaced innocent people are the greatest humanitarian challenge for our international community.

> The world is having a nervous breakdown. People are irritable, aggressive, tense, and anxious. Neurosis is on the march. It is galloping ahead at full speed and no one seems to know what is going on or why. Above all, no one seems to know how to stop this inexorable march to destruction. Year after year there is more illness, more suicide, more violence, more alcoholism and drug addiction. The world is coming apart at the seams. Valium is the glue holding it together.
>
> **—Dr Arthur Janov**

As a race, we are at the end of our tether and truly cannot continue to live in our current global social chaos, put up with our avoidable social pressures and endure to suffer more by serving and supporting the system that by design perpetuates our daily agonies. What have we done as a race to deserve such cruel treatment and what has happened to our brilliant human intelligence and ingenuity to show us the way forward?

Some of us in the west may say that life isn't that bad and question what all this fuss is about. It is true that <u>on the surface</u>, some of us may have it easier. We may have a job at present, have holidays every now and then and our life may not be in immediate danger today. However, since we are all systemically connected and subjected to the laws of cause and effect, whatever we may have right now is not necessarily going to be sustainable as we face the future, especially when we are serving the system that exists at the mercy of many disadvantaged people in this world. Therefore it does not matter where we live or how prosperous we may feel at present, we need to be conscious and socially participate in this global systemic world or we all going to pay for it one way or another through the systemic laws that we cannot escape from.

> One of the penalties for refusing to participate in politics is that you end up being governed by your inferiors.
>
> **—Plato**

The official explanations for our current social dilemmas often and conveniently point fingers at the symptoms or the innocents. For example, greedy and cruel human nature is often blamed for our current social crises or sometimes officials blame a bunch of disorganised ignorant war mongers wearing black pyjamas in the desert who for some magical reasons have become so miraculously organised, wealthy and powerful overnight.

The truth is that there has never ever been a plausible official explanation given to the masses that can intelligently enlighten them of the true nature and the root causes of why the world is the way it is – **dysfunctional and cruel**.

This book is aimed to enlighten those who are interested in knowing the truth about how humanity is currently positioned in our global social landscape, how they generally experience world events around them, what fuels the current social chaos and how it can be effectively changed to create a world of sustainable prosperity for all.

In the search for the truth, this book diligently examines our human journey in life, starting from birth and explores how we unconsciously become socially conditioned as we go through our learning experiences. It explains how, as newly born infants, we bring many wonderful innate qualities into life that are well worthy of careful preservation and intelligent nurturing. It reveals that through the course of our family and school education process, some of these cherished qualities become adversely impacted and sometimes lost altogether. In addition, we carefully examine how our life-lasting mental views are formed as we go through the process of learning and growing up.

The findings also reveal the main root causes of our social failing and unmask some of the quandaries we are confronted with as a race. We learn that our current social demise is totally avoidable and it is not happening by accident or due to organic accumulation of a series of innocent mistakes. It argues that our diabolical social problems are deliberately manufactured and engineered in order to create the chaotic social system we currently experience.

In order to search for real and lasting answers, this book takes the reader on a journey of self-discovery. It suggests that as we explore the nature of our human essence and understand our inner mental composition and beliefs, we slowly begin to develop our wisdom and become appropriately equipped to tackle a much larger task of changing the wider world.

We discover that our true freedom must begin within the confinement of our own mind and once we can create harmony and resolve our internal fights, then we can confidently project outwards and consciously reduce the external noise, create lasting peace with life and collectively prosper.

Finally and more inspirationally, this book explores what it means to be civilised and it offers potential solutions for how, as a deserving human race, we can reorganise ourselves and reclaim our place in history. It proposes a new social/ political architecture using peaceful and intelligent activities that are especially designed to cut through challenging social and political odds. It inspires people on how to become united and how to courageously demand their human rights and values from their respective authorities in a civilised and organised fashion.

I don't claim to have all the answers, however, to

the best of my ability, I projected conscious objectivity and stayed with the obvious and self-explanatory facts that should not be disputed by an average reader.

My reason for writing this book gradually evolved as I began to see clearer through the jigsaw puzzle of our social confusions, joined the dots between undisputed facts and also felt morally obliged to help raise awareness as a way of positively contributing to my fragile global society.

2

The Human Social Journey in Life

Stating the Obvious

We may not fully understand why we exist, what exactly we are meant to do in this life or how best to achieve it, but we can intelligently make certain factual deductions about things we witness around ourselves. If we look at life broadly and take careful stock of what we can observe, we may acknowledge the following to be true.

Our Natural Beginning

We come to this world with our unique personalities as well as other qualities which we commonly share with one another. As human beings, we are all programmed by nature to meet our survival needs by using our human intelligence to show us the way forward. Such intelligence allows us to explore life, learn, and adapt in order to improve our situations on an ongoing basis and better meet our needs.

Our Natural Ending
As mysteriously as we come to be, at some point in time, we leave this world. It is generally not clear what happens to us from that point onwards, but it is something we don't think much about until we find ourselves closer to the time of departure and see the urgency for some form of prior preparation. We generally don't look forward to dying due to its unknown or somewhat scary nature and also the reluctance for leaving behind what we love and are familiar with.

Evolution of knowledge through generations
As a race we have existed for thousands of years and over this period, we have accumulated and refined our overall knowledge about the world and its dynamic ecosystem. In general, each generation expands on the previous knowledge and passes their version of the truth to the next generation. Our assessment of the true nature of our physical world has fundamentally evolved from many superstitious views to a highly sophisticated and logically deduced interpretation of our defined reality. Through our great scientific understanding of the world, we have been able to dream and assemble everything we see around ourselves.

Application of human knowledge for the creation of our social structures
Our human society and our governing political bodies have also been evolving since our cave man days.

Our human social history is riddled with continuous failings by many governing groups attempting to bring about social cohesion and equitable prosperity for their citizens. The creation of a well thought out and designed society has been proven highly challenging for our governing leaders. As a technologically advanced race, we are unreasonably struggling to establish a civilised 21st century social structure. By and large almost all social systems have been failing to deliver to their people desired and balanced social outcomes. It seems that we somehow don't get along with each other or can't agree with certain social definitions or rules. We don't quite know why we are struggling so badly, especially in view of the opportunities we have had over millennia to learn, adapt and change whatever that is not working for us in life.

Why do we Need Social Organisation?

If you think about all existing human social organisations, especially those in earlier human history, you realise they all came to exist only for one simple reason – 'to benefit their members'. So the primary goal or the reason for any social organisation has to be prosperity for all its constituents. Therefore it is naturally expected that those who belong to such a social system are equitably looked after by the system. This should include the newly born children, weak and elderly with little or no physical ability to contribute to the system. That is why we are attracted to social organisational settings. We simply come together to collectively create better life for ourselves, because logically we know that social organisations should systemically be capable of providing social values more efficiently and effectively to their members than an individual living alone and attempting to do everything by themselves in the wild. The truth is that you can't create big opportunities and maximise prosperity all by yourself. The system always produces far more than the sum total of its individual outputs.

If you look at the most basic primitive social structure such as the family unit, the collaboration of family members makes it possible for them to survive better in the wild. For example, you could almost imagine in our ancestor's time the father sharpens his tools and goes hunting to feed his family, children help with chores like collecting wood and the mother maintains the hut and looks after the kids so at the end of the day, each member of the family could share and enjoy the warmth, food and shelter (Prosperity for ALL – This has always been the main purpose behind the most basic of earlier organised social structures).

Now if you look at most business organisations today, you quickly realise how much we have deviated and forgotten why we came together in the first place. For example, in our modern corporate settings, there is no such thing as prosperity for all and as a matter of fact what incentivises most corporations today is just pure greed and prosperity for a few at the expense of many. It is important to note that something is fundamentally wrong with our social structure as it continuously struggles to deliver or maintain civilised ways of living and deprives us from the joys of experiencing harmonious social coexistence.

Social concept of 'Us and them'
Life's natural processes and events always help to shape our social evolution, first by meeting our individual survival needs in life, then expanding to embrace the loved ones (such as children, relatives) and friends. We regard those who are important to us as part of our social organisation and try to exclude those who are perceived as threats, or those we regard as unimportant. We also draw mental boundaries and create clusters of relevancy and importance for members within our social organisation. When we draw a boundary, we make a clear statement where the border of our organisation, community or country actually is and who is in and who is out. Through such subjective means, we have divided the human race into manmade clusters with different rights and entitlements.

We often distinguish some social members belonging to the immediate inner circle (family) and others (such as friends, community, country, etc.), as belonging to the outer circles. Therefore, the boundary for the members and how significant they are within the social organisation can become highly subjective and very much dependent on the arbitrary boundaries we mentally create. For example, some environmentally friendly social organisations may embrace far more constituent members within their inner circle, than the greedy organisations with a handful of members in their inner circle. In general, people who are closer to the inner circle will benefit more than those on the outer circles. The social organisational responsibility can be intentionally expanded to include a much wider selection of constituencies such as the people and environment from the global perspective.

Influencing factors for choosing the inner circle members

The way we choose who should belong to the inner circle of our social structure is highly dependent on two important factors:

- The level of resources available and general abundance in our environment. More abundance and availability, less fears for us to see others as threats, more chance for us wanting to share with others, greater opportunity for us to shift focus more on our creative pursuits and less preoccupation with our basic survival needs. Conversely if we are worried about our basic survival due to resource scarcities, there is more chance we become less generous and less equitable with regards to the concept of prosperity for all.

- The more spiritually we evolve as individuals, the more capacity we develop to be inclusive and open our arms to embrace more people as part of ourselves. Conversely, if we are socially conditioned to be fearful, selfish or greedy, we could easily exclude and disproportionally sacrifice the majority for the sake of providing benefits to the minorities.

How to address our social dilemmas?

Our human social journey in this book encompasses a multitude of individual and shared experiences in life and in order to understand how these experiences shape us and influence the way we think and live, we need to carefully examine them with psychological, social and political lenses.

In order to rationally address our complex social quandaries and deliberately avoid the influences of our mental biases and our existing artificial social constructs, it is best to start right from the beginning and explore a typical child's developmental journey in life. We follow this journey by starting from birth and explore what qualities and tendencies a child may generally bring into this life and discover what could happen as the child evolves and becomes moulded by his/ her family and social ways or traditions.

As children we are extremely vulnerable as we always look up to authorities and people we trust most such as our parents, elders and official representatives such as teachers, police, doctors, etc. Since our perception of the world is still forming and our brain neural networks are massively expanding, especially in the first few years of our lives, we are learning fast and feeling hungry to absorb new experiences. We are totally reliant on the sensory information we receive from our environment.

The key area for us to investigate is how we are mentally shaped in different social settings and conditioned by our conventional educational systems. We also explore in detail what educational practices mean in terms of their contents validity and how they may change and reshape us for our future social challenges.

Finally we look into how we may end-up having our particular experiences in life as adults and discover how we may intelligently review and change what does not holistically serve us.

3.

What innate potential children possess

In this section, we shall explore some of the basic drivers and qualities in children at the earliest stage of their lives.

The natural process of life for the evolution of a foetus in the womb ensures that the baby is anchored and innately programmed by nature to have the following basic needs and characteristics in life:

- We are programed at the time of birth to be driven to meet and satisfy our human needs on an ongoing basis, once we are born and set foot into this life. We are calibrated with our innate intelligence for learning and adapting to our new world within the boundaries and allowances of our natural ecosystem and environment. At the early stage of life, up to age 5, children create around 18 million neurons in their brains per minute. Such developmental evolution helps them to progressively advance their cognitive capabilities at this stage.

- We are programed to crave to belong. The sense of belonging in children creates a need for them wanting to be part of a family and larger communities (this is the natural expansion of our wider self).
- We individually bring to life a unique identity that differentiates us from one another. The sense of individual purpose is part of this uniqueness. Our life Purpose, even though it is not always consciously obvious to us at our individual level, is part of what drives us towards certain directions and endeavours in life.

Some facts at the initial stage of a child's life

This is about <u>who</u> we are and <u>what</u> our true essence is at the early stage of life.

Apart from children's individual and distinct personalities, the following qualities are commonly shared by most children at the early stage of their lives. In my personal view, these qualities are the most precious assets we possess in life and we must preserve them at any cost as our true essence for happiness directly depends on them.

- **Closer to the experience of oneness** – At the very early stages in life, children have no real understanding of their <u>sense of self</u>. They can't distinguish between themselves and their environment. They have no idea where they actually begin or end. To them it is just one continuum of life without any differentiation or subdivision of objects around them. The sense of conscious awareness for the concept of self-recognition forms later in their lives.

- **Honest expression of their feelings** – Children only respond to <u>pleasure and pain</u>. If something engages them and makes them happy they keep doing and if something makes them unhappy they react and complain about it. They don't play politics or mind games. Without any clichés, they express how they feel and say it 'how they see it'.

- **Life is exciting to them** – The prospect of <u>life is exciting</u> and full of things they don't know as they feel intensely <u>alive</u> and busy to explore their world almost as a scientist would. They have a real <u>spark of life</u> in them. Life is out there to be discovered. To them life is generally full of things they don't know and things they want to investigate in every corner. I am sure many of us can relate to that, especially as we get older and feel that we have lost some of that spark in ourselves.

- **Have simple needs in life** – They are <u>easily pleased</u> with simple things as they have not yet been introduced to the concept of consumerism. By and large a child even in a most basic environment <u>can be happy</u> as long as they are engaged and fed.

- **Stimulated & inquisitive** – They love stimulation & interaction on their own terms and as much as they can manage at the time. They are highly inquisitive to learn. For example, they empty a rubbish bin and become fascinated by what they might find in it and as you can guess, objects usually end up in their mouths for a quick taste and validation of their usefulness.

- **Open to possibilities** – They <u>don't apply limitations</u> upon themselves as they can go right to the edge of a cliff, just to see what is on the other side. <u>Everything is possible for them</u>. I remember as a very small child, to my parent's horror, I used to climb a tall cabinet, sit on top of it and play with my toys.

- **Courageous** – They don't have our <u>conventional fears</u> about the world around them. They have no fear about <u>making mistakes</u> or doing things outside normal conventions or social contexts.

- **Highly Imaginative** – They are highly imaginative and take <u>pleasure in their creativity</u>. For example, they turn a cardboard box into an imaginary car and draw amazing shapes that they can relate to. I believe children at this earlier age have some special connections with their world and can potentially visualise things that adults place limitations on.

- **Follow no social rules** – They act naturally as they are <u>not socially conscious</u> and social rules are not known to them as yet. For example, they can freely do whatever they want to do without worrying about what other people may think. The presence of a king or a queen makes no difference to them in what they are about to do.

- **Trusting** – They <u>trust most</u> things as they don't have preconceived ideas about anything. This sense of trust stops them worrying about their physical selves and at the same time encourages them to keep on exploring and learning without fears.

- **Look up to Authorities & Social Role Models** – They respect and look up to their <u>guardians</u> and <u>authorities</u> and see them as role models. This is due to the sense of trust they place on the world around themselves and they don't need to be preoccupied with basic survival (such as where their next meal is coming from) because they trust that authorities know and will provide. For a child, the concept of authority becomes directly synonymous with the notion of 'knowledge and power'. For this reason, any person in a position of power will automatically become a role model candidate to a soul searching child.

4.

How we are shaped at home within the family context

In this section we examine how we are developed by our parents within the context of the family environment. We discuss how our parents work hard to instil in us what they subjectively believe to be appropriate and teach us social behaviours that can help us with our individual development in life. There are many wonderful qualities that parents give us, especially those that are aligned with the concept of human decency and how one should uphold certain important values in life.

According to their individual prior learning and experience, parents unconsciously try to inspire certain beliefs and behaviours in us that, in the hindsight, could be viewed as inappropriate or potentially unworthy for us to retain. Some such unwise beliefs and views could even play adverse roles in our adult life. I am sure at some level we can all relate to such things. For example, fear based beliefs or obsessions about things or certain narrow perspectives that perhaps did not sound right to us even at an early stage of our lives.

My focus here is not placed on those wise qualities we were given by our parents, as those instilled beliefs often speak for themselves and do not need to be mentioned in this book. I am deliberately trying to pick on certain conditioning that could potentially have negative future connotations in life for us and that we need to become aware of and understand their ramifications especially when it comes to teaching and helping our own children in life.

Some facts about the parent's teaching role within the family context:

- The parents' intention for their children is to educate them the best way possible so they can survive and thrive going forward in their lives.
- The way in which we create and define our roles in the family constellation is a <u>manmade construct</u> which is often passed on from one generation to another. The facts and quality of information that we are taught as children within the family cluster is highly dependent on the wisdom of our parents at the time.
- Parents with the best intentions, try to instil in their children what they believe to be in line with <u>social expectations</u> and provide subjective ways of how a child should live and interact with the world around him/ her in order to be successful;
- The way parents provide education varies from one family to another based on their own

childhood upbringing and their social conditioning. For example, some parents may apply the rewards & punishments method and others may use experiential methods for teaching their children. Some parents manage this with a tight grip of control and with little tolerance for mistakes and become highly critical. At the other extreme, some parents may be too lenient, forgiving or soft.

- As the primary carers, parents have a unique advantage in how they can influence their children. Based on the laws of creation and natural programing, most children innately want to please their parents and consequently, they try to do as much as possible to align with their parents' ways. The only time they may rebel against their parents' desires is when they see imposed expectations upon them which are beyond their ability to comply and that is when they are likely to rebel in order to preserve their own sanity.

Parents teach children 'how not to miss out on meeting their needs in life'

With the best of intentions, parents teach their children:

1. **Harnessing parental values and beliefs:** children are expected to embrace <u>values and beliefs</u> which their parents often subscribe to. Parents also promise that the adoption of such beliefs

and values by their children will result in them becoming more accepted and rewarded within the overall context of our social system. Parents do what they can to prepare their children for the future and provide them with their key experiences and what they know and have learnt from their own parents and their own general personal life experiences.

As we grow up and reflect back on early training by our parents, with the greatest respect to them, we often wonder how much they actually knew in terms of their worldly views, spiritual depth and material awareness that directly went into the process of shaping us for future challenges. We sometimes realise that many things we were taught by the elders may have come from unsound and dubious origins and may even be quite unsustainable in today's practices. This is not a blanket statement about condemning every parent or every lesson we were taught, I am merely expressing that not all our parents' points of view were necessarily correct or appropriate, as in many cases they just shared what they knew to be true.

Therefore, we are truly at the mercy of the maturity/wisdom of our parents and society at large. More open parents are in their outlooks, have a broader life perspective and understanding of the dynamics of their environment; there is a greater chance that their wider world views and knowledge could translate into what they teach their children. In such circumstances, children are more likely to become exposed to wiser/ fit for purpose perspectives that can subsequently help them to benefit from their earlier training, experiences and exposure to life. Conversely, the more misguided our parents are, more suffering we encounter, mainly due to their lack of openness and misaligned attitude to life.

Some children could even inherit some unwise tendencies from their parents in spite of the fact that they could have initially frowned on such behaviour. For example, a child who may have hated his father's unfair attitude towards others may grow up and unconsciously exercise similar traits in adult life. Of course we can always cleanse ourselves from any unwise earlier beliefs at a later date in life. That is if we first realise the need for change and choose to do so.

2. **Meaning of Self-worth:** Parents teach their children how to measure their self-worth both as a human being and as a member of society. Based on our shared social beliefs, the most common measure for self-worth is often defined as our <u>successes and failures in life</u>. In other words many parents categorically teach their children to have limited allowance or tolerance for making mistakes in their lives. According to many parents such human slippage is generally frowned upon by society and not regarded as an acceptable or successful human behaviour.

What is important to realise here is that the only way <u>we ever learn in life</u> is by having permission to <u>freely experiment</u> with our world and make <u>as many mistakes</u> as needed until we eventually get it right.

A person who never made a mistake never tried anything new.

—Albert Einstein

If we try to avoid making mistakes, especially when we subconsciously conditioned to do so at any cost (as is often wrongly preached in our society), we can never truly learn or do anything new in life. If our worthiness is measured by our success and failure in life, then we set a dangerous pace for our children to follow as they may develop a sense of low self-perception and feel unworthy, especially when they fail achieving things as per their parental expectations. Unfortunately suicide is the extreme case, where a person despairs so much and feels totally unworthy to even want to live and sadly may end up taking his or her life.

Tragically, the truth that we are never told in society is that 'our self-worth has absolutely nothing to do with our success or failure in life'. Our self-worth is about our convictions and what we demonstrate to ourselves with our ability to just keep on trying out new things in life and allowing ourselves to make as many mistakes as necessary so we can organically learn and grow based on our endeavours and trials.

3. **Teaching the concept of guilt:** Children are told that if they <u>break the rules</u> they are <u>guilty</u> and will be subjected to a measured punishment. The rules that we are expected to uphold as children often relate to parental personal values and beliefs. In general, values are our guidelines but unfortunately, we often break them due to other competing values and beliefs. For that reason when we compromise on our values, which we often do, we feel guilty.

   Example-1: You may dearly uphold a personal value of <u>Kindness</u> in your life, but yet another value such as <u>fairness</u> may cause you to act unkindly to someone who is unfair to you. In this scenario, your personal value of kindness is compromised by your action and consequently you feel guilty for being unkind in trying to uphold the personal Value of fairness.

   Example-2: Let's say, you highly subscribe to the concept of honour as an important value in your life. You may just as equally value the importance of family in your life. Now imagine that your sense of honour at work has been tested as your boss expects you to act dishonourably to support her clandestine cause. Now you have a choice to make. Your preferred choice might be to hand in your resignation and walk out honourably, however, you have a family to feed and jobs are really scarce.

What choice would you make knowing that if you walk out, your family could seriously suffer? Regardless of which choice you make, it will most likely be based on the interplay, strengths and priorities of these values at work. You cannot avoid feeling guilty because in this example, you end up compromising on one of your values (Family or Honour).

What does guilt mean and can we really be guilty? Guilt means that a person has consciously chosen to break a socially agreed rule so consequently, the person should pay for his/ her decision and action. The payment could be in terms of sacrifices the guilty person has to endure such as financial fines, imprisonment or physical suffering. Justice is about finding who is guilty and delivering punishment in order to restore the sense of fairness. Unconsciously, we are so familiar with how the whole process of guilt and punishment works that we sometimes adopt it to make people feel guilty when we want them to do something for us. In such a situation, the experience of guilt (the proposition that a person will be guilty in future) which we place on a person to do something for us, reminds the person of the consequence of breaking those values which they uphold. We project to them their future experience of feeling guilty if they refuse to cooperate with us right now. Soon, they feel the sense of guilt begin to creep in and shortly after, they will submit to whatever was requested of them.

Are we really guilty as charged or is there another way of looking at this? As mentioned earlier, guilt implies that we have a free will to choose and somehow we consciously decide to break our conventional rules or expectations. If we examine this statement, we notice there are two key parts that we need to consider closely; 1) having a free will to choose, and 2) making wrong decisions.

All our decisions in life are ultimately made to enable and protect what matters to us in this ever-changing world. Decisions are made based on what we hold internally as subjective truth. This truth is based on our beliefs and priorities that allow us to interpret the world, decide and pursue a particular course of action.

If our beliefs are ultimately responsible for our final decisions, then where does free will come from and where does it get its powers to override the views of our predictable core beliefs that subconsciously drive us?

What does free will really mean? It means that our conscious mind is sharp, unbiased and focused enough to stay independent of subconscious influences and can objectively make its own decisions. The truth is that when we decide, most of us become quickly overpowered by the body's emotional and chemical changes generated by our subconscious. Subjective interpretations of the way the subconscious views reality, influence us all the way to the core of our mental and physical being. Its message is delivered through generated emotions that reach us at a cellular level. It is similar to being injected with drugs or alcohol and still being told that we have free will and we should just ignore the influences of the drug on our minds and bodies. Of course this is a false statement as the drug in our system will reduce conscious objectivity, dilute our judgment and reduce the potential for the concept of free will to have a chance to operate. In the same way, we can never have free will.

Example; Imagine we have a baby boy just being born and miraculously we can create an identical replica of him immediately after his birth. Now we have two absolutely identical children. What happens if we place one of them in a horrid and brutal environment, where the poor child is systemically exposed to daily physical abuse, humiliation, hunger and mental deprivation?

The other boy we place in the best possible family in the best part of the world. This family can provide the ultimate potential for this boy. They give him unconditional love 24 x 7. They offer him quality education and appropriate socialisation. They teach him well-rounded and worldly wisdom, and how to interact with life.

Now years have gone by and these boys are grown men. One boy perhaps ends up being a great social figure who would like to help vulnerable people or he might be a well to do and committed physician.

On the other hand, the other boy might be dealing in drugs and burglaries to survive. He might even become a contract killer to pay his way.

The question for us here is – is this man guilty for being a drug dealer or a cold blooded killer? How come his identical replica is doing so well and so differently? The successful replica man now works for a humanitarian organisation and would never dream of being a drug dealer or hurting anyone.

Since we have removed the variability of **nature** as both children have exactly the same nature, the only influencing factor is now the **nurture**. So if we agree that our environment makes us what we are today and continues to govern our future decisions and actions, surely for this man to be guilty, he must be responsible for choosing his awful environment as a boy! Are we therefore responsible for the environment that surrounds us and acts upon us? Did the boys choose to be in either situation – the well to do family or the brutal one? Without any consultation, he was simply born to a family, a community and a given geography. The rest just happened to him.

This should remind those of us on high horses who boast how well and proper we are in our lives. Please Just change places with those who are really having it hard, brutalised all their lives and desperate to survive. Now please witness how much of your shine comes off and if you would end up acting any differently to those unfortunate people.

For the sake of simplicity, I deliberately don't wish to open up the debate and bring in the concept of past life possibilities that indicate: – how we may come here to experience what we are supposed to experience. Quantum Mechanics also advocates that we create our own reality or at least we have a lot to do with it. We discuss these later in the book.

I certainly subscribe to the fact that we all do things we may regret afterwards and we often feel bad because we have compromised our values to some degree, but **no one is really guilty** as guilt implies that we have this glorified notion of free will – an independent observer who stands above us and is totally untouched by our subconscious influences. Let's do the following exercise to see how the concept of free will becomes so hard to apply.

Exercise: Do you like to be happy or sad in life? If your answer is 'I prefer to be happy' and you also believe that you have a clear cut free will to choose whatever you wish, please use your great magic of free will and choose never to be sad, angry, fearful or never break any of your values. See if you can bring such a decision into action through your so called free will. If you find it hard to achieve this, you will realise that your so called free will is not that free after all.

The problem in teaching children a sense of guilt as a normal day-to- day condition is that we set them up to constantly and often uncontrollably pouring out their anger and punishment on themselves and others around them. A continual experience of guilt does not serve us well in life as it robs us of our peace of mind and damages our physical health. We definitely should learn from our mistakes and refine our thoughts and beliefs as we go forward, but we should never embrace guilt. We can say to ourselves that 'I did what I knew at that time and based on my level of knowing'. Then we should say that we have learnt from it, change our ways and we are grateful for experiencing such potential for learning.

Guilt is the root of many human psychological miseries & evils in life.

To know whether we feel guilty or not about a situation, we can test ourselves after we encounter a situation where one of our personal values such as honesty, responsibility, kindness, etc., is being compromised. For example; somebody may be robbing an old lady right in front of you. In such a situation, your personal values such as honesty and kindness are clearly compromised in this situation and your value that upholds Kindness indicates to you that by such standards, the robber is guilty. If you could, you would intervene and restore justice and punish the perpetrator for your own sense of pleasure by restoring justice. However, he is much bigger and uglier than you and he also looks very mean. So your desire to punish the guilty man for being unkind, dishonest and definitely irresponsible is now quashed and your personal value for 'self-preservation' has won. Therefore ashamed (feeling guilty) for not intervening in the situation, you just watch in horror and after wards when he has fled, you go to the assistance of the old lady.

Later in the day when you get home, you sit and think about the event. Now you must ask yourself 'do I feel guilty'? Say to yourself 'I only did what I could' and if in future I ever learn self-defence, I might do it differently in similar situations, but for now, that was all I could have done' and I am going to consciously feel at peace with myself as I have done nothing wrong. If you still feel a sense of anger towards the person or the situation, it may imply a sense of guilt within you. The interesting thing is that you see the perpetrator as a coward for attacking a weak defenceless person and at the same time you also see yourself as a coward for not defending the old lady. So in reality most of that anger is for your own perceived shortfalls.

4. **Be competitive:** Parents want their kids to look out for themselves in this wild world and they tell them that they have to climb up the ladder of success while others are left behind or stepped over. It is true that our social designers greatly

advocate the concept of competition as the main ingredient for social prosperity. That is how we have all been raised **'to be the winner'**, and **'not the loser'**. But is it wise to be competitive in life? Is being competitive the right recipe for a sustainable and effective society? Our intelligence helps us to learn from nature; for example, if the cells in your body begin to compete with one another in one area of your body, what will eventually happen to your body as time goes on? Of course, what quickly comes to mind is physical disharmony and disease. What happens to our communities if people are competing rather than collaborating? What happens to our organisations when employees are competing with each other rather than learning and openly sharing with each other what they know towards a common goal?

As part of their teachings on competitiveness, parents also let us believe that being independent in life is a normal human condition. What does 'independent' actually mean? Being independent teaches us the culture of not asking for help or collaborating with one another for better or more holistic results. It also assumes that we have enormous energy reserves at our disposals that can be unleashed to do everything for ourselves so we don't need to reach out to others for help.

The concept of independence is not an achievable expectation for parents to place on their children. Such a belief could cause children to lose confidence in things they may potentially need help with or they might think that they are less capable than those imaginary super independent people that their parents have painted in their imaginations. I don't know about you, but I need help as I can't do and don't want to do everything by myself. Instead, of teaching children to be independent, they should really be taught to enjoy themselves while they are doing their share in society (ND Greg Neville – Teaching on Illnesses & Psychosomatic System).

People achieve far more through co-operation and mutual interaction, than competitively outdoing one another or doing it alone. This is the nature of the systemic world that we are currently living in and we had better get used to living harmoniously and collaboratively for the common good of all. Professor Dacher Keltner's research (UC Berkeley) reveals that as a race, we are far more cooperative and caring than competitive. He also explains how Charles Darwin's work was tragically misrepresented to the masses. What most people remember from Darwin is that – human beings are competitive by nature and are mainly driven by the notion of 'survival of the fittest instinct'. What they don't hear is that Darwin extensively talked about the importance of animal cooperation in nature and rarely talked about the survival of the fittest.

5. **Work on your ability:** Children are often reminded how inadequate they are in their current capabilities and that they need to work hard to improve themselves. From maths to English or chemistry, whether they have aptitude for them or not. We often tell children that it is just not good enough and they must try harder to be successful. Some parents are so critical that inadvertently, they push their kids so hard they give up on the concept of living up to their parent's image and lose confidence in their capabilities. Sometimes by simply thinking that they have failed to please their parents, they may stop trying and even become rebellious and awkward. Imagine people force you to become a good accountant when you don't like, enjoy or have an aptitude for accounting and as it happens, you are a great medical doctor and at the peak of your career working to cure cancer. There is really nothing wrong with our abilities, it is more about beliefs and priorities that we need to focus and improve on. Our beliefs dictate how we conduct ourselves in life (refer Greg Neville's work).

6. **Make good decisions:** Parents often remind their children to try to make the best possible decisions they can in their daily interactions with life. They also tell their children that if they deliberately make wrong decisions, they will be labelled 'guilty' and 'responsible' for the outcomes. Once again, parents mean well, but how much truth is in what

we preach to our children? Can we intentionally make bad decisions in life? It is true that from time to time, we regret our decisions, especially those that do not serve us, but do we consciously spend energy to make <u>bad decisions</u> in the first place and if so, what is the point of doing that?

The truth is that we DO NOT make bad decisions EVER; we make the best possible decisions at any given moment based on our current beliefs/ wisdom, priorities and needs. Of course in hindsight, we are always much wiser, but at the time we make a decision, we always do the best we can. Basically the mental process of decision making is always the same in every human being. The thing that varies from one person to the next is the quality of the beliefs, relevancy of our driving needs and priorities that we individually hold at a given time. In short, the wiser our beliefs are, the better the quality of our decision and potential for unfolding rewards. However, at the time we make decisions, we generally do not drop our current beliefs and suddenly adopt better quality beliefs on the spot. This is not generally how it works. Such untruthful advice from parents can cause more anxiety for children than is necessary.

7. **Work Harder:** Children are often told not to be lazy and work harder to achieve things in life. They are told the harder they work, the more they shall succeed and ultimately will be happier in life. Basically children are told '**if you are good, you**

will get'. If you comply, you will succeed. Work within the parameters. Don't question or shake things too much.

It is true that our effort often equates to what we generally achieve in life, but I totally disagree with the comment that people can be lazy out of choice. We just do what is in the scope of our beliefs and priorities. For example; as a vegetarian, you may not be as proactive or enthusiastic working in a butcher shop or as a teenager with great interest to attend parties with friends; you may not be as motivated mowing the lawns at home for your father. However, given the chance, you may surf all day long or dance all night long in a night club. We just serve our beliefs and priorities and nothing else. So therefore, it is impossible for us to work harder at any given time.

8. **Fear of missing out:** Parents often instil in their children the most unnecessary and stressful fear based belief that they could miss out in life if they are not careful. This is done with best intentions as a way of getting them to become more conscious of not missing out on potential opportunities that life may offer them. I am sure some of you relate to phrases such as:' If you don't go to school, you will be no one' or 'if you don't look after yourself, nobody is going to marry you', etc. On close ex-amination, establishment of such fear based traits does not serve our children well in life. What is wrong with the concept of missing out? Anything

we ever do in life is based on what we know and are able to do at that time. Therefore by such a viewpoint, if what we do is the only thing we can do, there is no way we can force ourselves to do something outside of our given paradigm and frame of thinking as it would be totally impossible and illogical. Therefore it is totally wrong to suggest that someone could actually miss out on anything in life as life always tends to give us the appropriate experience of diverse and often unpleasant nature at exactly the right time and place for our specific growth and development in life. Of course in hindsight, we may think that we should have done something else, but there is no way we would have known that. Therefore fear of missing out does not change anything at all and as a matter of fact it would have the opposite effect by actually making us more doubtful and incapacitate us from acting promptly and taking advantage of situations in life when we should.

Children's perspective

By the end of the parental home education process, children, to various degrees, become exposed and shaped into commonly endorsed social behaviours and expectations. The following experiences are likely to occur:

1. As children become moulded, their initial **sense of openness to their world** rightly or wrongly **closes** somewhat as they buy into social beliefs. Their

creative light for free expression somewhat dims as they fit into new social ways.

2. The children's focus slowly shifts towards feeling more **fearful** and **stressed** about how they may <u>comply</u> with the new set of expectations and become <u>**competitive**</u> in life.

3. **Contradictions and double standards.** Due to contradictions and inconsistencies we observe about our parents' behaviour, we start to become suspicious of their wisdom and subsequently begin to mistrust some of their advice and teaching topics. Some of you may remember when many parents used to tell their children not to smoke and how bad cigarettes are while they were puffing away on their own cigarettes.

5.

How we are shaped
and moulded at school

The school system follows on from our parents' earlier teachings and provides a socially structured program in order to open children to sciences, social rules and practical knowledge of how to progress in the world. Our teachers are generally highly dedicated, under resourced and often underpaid individuals. Their work is highly structured and scrutinised by the system in order to maintain uniform standards of education for our young ones. Teachers are seldom allowed to tailor their teaching materials to address specific areas of needs. They are also restricted in including their own personal worldly wisdom into their teaching practices. Teachers are social instruments for passing on what is set in concrete as standard social educational agendas and practices. Such standards reflect the current wisdom of our scientific, social and governmental institutions.

Some facts about the learning experience within the school context:

- In theory, our school system is expected to help prepare children for life, help them to effectively meet their needs in society and learn how to create and live within the family and a larger communities context;

- Historically speaking, for many generations, our educational systems were focused on the content propagation of knowledge, rather than the intellectual deduction of solutions to life's problems. It somehow failed to help young adults to develop a cognitive process for deriving the required behaviour for addressing their life challenges. Our education system has evolved since, however, it still lacks the necessary provisions for teaching children how to adapt when they are dealing with the ongoing world of change & variability, that is, how to intelligently anticipate and respond to situations. It is still more about tools, methods and end-to-end static processes. It is mainly about the application of readymade formulas to situations rather than the ability to think at will for intelligent and workable solutions;

- In order to equip and sharpen children's sense of social belonging and the sense of social achievements in life, Parents push children to be educated at school where these messages are reinforced. The parent's high expectations of their children to do well at school are pro-gressively getting worse, especially over the last few decades as some new age parents are pushing their kids harder than ever before. It is almost like an obsession for their children to do better than other kids which obviously translates to much longer hours of study and extra curriculum at school in order for their kids to achieve the Super-Kid status and learn to become competitive.

Therefore the shoehorn fitting and moulding of our children into school and society is based on social standards reinforced by the author-ities, parents and school. Remember parents themselves are heavily influenced and condi-tioned by their social norm of 'More competi-tive you become, more successful you become'. For this reason parents feel compelled to push their kids harder and harder to become smarter and comply quicker. They just inno-cently reinforce their social fears upon their children. For example, Kids in many Asian countries, such as Korea sometimes don't get home until night time. So what happened to the childhood play time and the idea that real strength comes through organic growth rather than hasty and unnatural processes?

- Children have trust in the wisdom of authori-ties, especially in the way such views often get enforced by our parents. In society, we idealise and believe that experts have the right formula for success. Therefore teachers are to be trusted so children can directly benefit from their teachings and wisdom. Children especially at a young age try to mimic their teachers because they think teachers have real answers. Teachers are their important role models.

- As children, while we are learning, to a greater extent, we are protected and supported by our parents and not totally exposed to the dynamic brunt of social forces as yet. For this reason as kids we still enjoy some of the freedom we are entitled to.

Teachers teach children 'how not to miss out on meeting their needs in life'

With the best intentions, teachers teach children to conform to what parents have already been pushing them to follow – not to miss out on meeting their needs in life and to be fully conscious of 'the fear of missing out on things in life':

- A set of beliefs that we need to have in order to be accepted within the social system;
- To measure our <u>self-worth</u> based on our <u>successes and failures</u>, in other words **limited allowances** for **mistakes** in life;
- If we make a bad decision and <u>break the rules</u> we are <u>guilty</u> and subject to punishment;
- To be strong and **to cope** with things in life and soldier on;

- To **be independent** and stand on our own feet;
- To **be competitive** or we will be **swallowed up by competitors**;
- **Don't make mistakes** and **always shine**;
- **Work on your ability** because you don't have enough of it.
- You have to **work harder** to succeed. The harder you work the more success you achieve.
- We **have real choices** that we can make at any time in our lives.
- **If you are good, you will get**. If you **comply** you will **succeed**. Work within the parameters. Don't question or shake things too much.

Children's Perspective:

By the end of the education process, children become exposed, and to a great degree, moulded into the wisdom of the social norm. Some children may rebel at this point due to either:

1. their general frustrations and disillusionment with the sanity of the 'rule prescribing authorities'. The ones, who in children's views, fraudulently claim to have real solutions and recipes for good social management, endorsed rules for correct social behaviours to deliver predictable life outcomes;

2. their personal sense of failing in living up to standards and expectations set for them by the authorities (i.e. parents, teachers). Remember that kids, by nature always like to please their

parents and people around them. However if they fail to please, they progressively evolve to eventually rebel as a way of saving face and reclaim some of their sense of dignity.

The children who remain compliant with their social expectation are likely to experience the following:

1. Children **become moulded even further now** into social acceptance and beliefs that are deemed by teachers and the education system as acceptable and appropriate social behaviours;

2. Their sense of **openness to their world often closes even further** for them buying more and more into the wisdom of their teachers and parents' sets of belief. Their **creativity** <u>dims</u> even further as they mentally fit more into the prescribed mould of how to be and how to act;

3. Their **focus moves** further and further to be <u>more fearful of their world</u> and they become more **stressed** for trying to be **compliant and competitive** even if they don't deeply feel right about this;

4. **Contradictions and double standards.** Due to contradictions and inconsistencies within the school and broader society, their suspicions about authority's wisdom will increase and subsequently their **mistrust for authorities will grow** stronger.

5. **Disillusionment of what is right.** The process of disillusionment begins. As children we start to really lose trust. We start to disrespect authorities for their lack of knowhow and pretending to have the right answers. This is where children could become more rebellious towards authority.

6.

Application of our acquired learning in a social/community context

This is when young adults join the workforce for the first time, which by today's standard, is a great privilege. This is when their previous learning and the benefits of their upbringing are given the real opportunity to be exercised and tested in REAL WORLD situations. Now through their mental/ physical exertions and contributions to their world, they are in a position to generate real rewards for themselves.

In theory our social designers want us to buy into their social rules so in their beliefs, we can achieve more success and happiness in our lives. Here we are – trained by our parents, teachers and communities and ready to put to use our worldly wisdom and practice what we have learnt to create a happy life for ourselves and our wider world.

Entering the work force

So what experiences can employers, organisations and communities give or reinforce in us while we function within their jurisdictions and management practises? We were told how things are in life and how they work. Now here is the test to validate our learning while we pursue happiness. The following are some of the undesired experiences we may encounter during our working phase.

Competitiveness & mistakes

- We are openly encouraged to have fire in our bellies at work, as if we are meant to go to war with others, such as colleagues who are also trying hard to get more shine than us and succeed before we do. As part of our social promotion of the competitive working culture, generally in the recruitment selection process, candidates are often asked if they have fire in their bellies in order to push themselves harder for success.

- We are measured by our successes and even more punished for our mistakes. Now as adults we pay dearly for our mistakes than as children. The pressure is now on for us to stay squeaky clean and avoid mistakes. In truth the preservation of our external image and trying to constantly look good, limit us from experiencing a relaxed self-expressive journey in life, making it more detrimental to our sense of spontaneity, creativity and manifestation.

- How do we learn? Of course, by making mistakes. So how can we learn if making mistakes is not accepted as a social norm? The social notion of 'we must avoid mistakes' comes from our more fundamental earlier social conditionings. For this reason we all try very hard to be socially good so we can benefit and receive handsomely from it. That is why our social image is so important to us. We want to show our best side to the public and we hide our weaknesses. The common social belief of 'if you are good, you will get' means that if you fail, you can't be that good. So therefore you are advised if you want to receive well from life, <u>you cannot make mistakes</u>. That is why we are all desperately trying to fit in, deliver as expected and be good. There is no room for failure in our lives as that is regarded as a sign of weakness.

These restrictive beliefs within us cause a great deal of damage and stifle our creativity which is our only tool for reaching true happiness and prosperity in life.

Contradiction and confusion
- What we as young adults have learnt from our elders and teachers does not match the reality of life we actually face. Life seems to be much more dynamic and complex for the application of the simple rules and formulas we have learnt.

- Because of the contradictions, double standards and incompleteness in our social and professional wisdom, we start losing our sense of trust with authority figures who keep on failing to be effective and provide sustainable and equitable solutions to the society that they are meant to manage.
- Because of the pressures imposed on us, we are more likely to lose our confidence by feeling not able to service all our constituencies as a well as we would like. Therefore, we doubt and often harshly judge ourselves and think the worse which means our confidence is taking a beating.

We question our abilities rather than question the rules

We begin to believe that the level of our performance is directly related to the amount of ability we possess. We have learnt that if we are not getting ahead in life, it is because somehow we are failing to utilise or comply with prescribed social rules. We come to the conclusion that it must be our personal abilities that are letting us down or perhaps result in our substandard behaviours. Then, we start to doubt our confidence and begin to blame our abilities.

Since we are so preoccupied with what we have been taught by society, without much thinking or serious questioning, we begin to doubt our own abilities.

Disillusionment

- Because of our ongoing experiences of social contradictions commonly exercised by our role models, the process of disillusionment about our so called 'experts' begins to take stronger root within us. We see there are different rules for different people and situations. We become aware of different camps, classes and the real meaning of the values that our role models publically uphold and somehow privately dismiss. Therefore in simple terms, we realise the jungle still rules in our social vein, but it is hardly ever seriously acknowledged or openly questioned by the mainstream authorities.

- We start to really lose trust in the wisdom of our leaders and their social intelligence. We become fearful and confused where to go and who to trust. This becomes more about authority's lack of competence and our lack of trust in them. For strange reasons, innocent human beings often get the short stick when it comes to the question of equitability and fair distribution of social rewards. Our authority seems to either lack greater wisdom or deliberately set out to exploit humanity. In either case, our system and our rule makers appear to have collectively failed to behave and deliver intelligently, fairly or caringly for their constituencies. For these reasons, we may start to disrespect them to a greater degree than before (as a young child)

- Unfortunately we quickly start noticing that in our formal society and mainstream practices, there are not many alternative views or solutions offered to us – the type of solutions that could potentially help us to address these fundamental social issues and problems. There are not many places for us to go for real help as most interesting new perspectives seem to have great applications within their own particular silos, boundaries and definitions, but somehow lose their real shine when they are viewed holistically or cross referenced with other silos (micro applications do not meet the need of the macro structure).

- In the main, by working in the social machinery called organisations, we may make some progress in meeting our physical and survival needs. However, many will struggle to fully experience and meet that deep sense of purpose or deep joy of real accomplishments. In spite of our social status and material achievements, for some, it feels as if something very important is missing from their lives and often they can't pin point what exactly those things are. One could argue that our physical and survival needs may be satisfied at the expense of our other deeper psychological and life needs. We become so preoccupied with creating a comfortable and better life for our bodies that sometimes we forget why we are here and what we are meant to contribute to this world. We need to become re-awakened, take stock and also realise the price we are paying for achieving such material gains, which in many cases, we could easily do without.

- The level of individual unhappiness, stress and dissatisfaction with the way we are interacting with life will increase. We experience disappointment with our failures, lack of progress and effectiveness. Our training somehow is not a great match for what we actually encounter in our social and working lives. There are many unanswered questions for us.

- We feel betrayed by inadvertently allowing ourselves to be programmed by so-called wise people and experts. Even though as children we had no conscious freedom to choose our guardians and leaders, we feel resentful of the level of misguidance we have received about many facets of our lives.

Some facts about us, now grown up, to act as a parent within our own family context:

In society we are trained to initially start life by just feeding ourselves and gradually expanding our sense of self to form larger families and communities.

We basically continue to do as our parents have done, i.e. raise our kids more or less in a similar socially conformist manner. We use similar socially manmade roles to define and shape our family units.

Again, as parents with the best of intentions for

our kids, we try to instil in them what we believe social expectations are and how our children should live and interact with the world around them. The sense of unhappiness will continue.

Our experiences of adulthood

- Without doubt, parents in general, love their children and enjoy the experience of watching them growing up. However, even though they may feed and take care of what matters to them (their children and spouses), their <u>personal sense of purpose</u> and satisfaction often may not be fully realised. As mentioned earlier, from our perspective of systemic principles for human interactions, our sense of purpose is not <u>just</u> about taking care of ourselves or our extended families; it is more about what we are meant to contribute to others and the wider world.

- At some later stage in our lives, many of us question <u>this lingering void</u> in our lives and it may even become a big worry for us as we feel less and less satisfied with life. Something is just missing even though on the surface we may have everything. We may even confuse ourselves by continuing more and more with our sense of dissatisfaction with things that we may not even be able to clearly articulate or recognise as the root causes of our problems. This can cause prolonged fatigue and stress in our mental and physical systems.

- We may feel as if we are <u>trapped</u> within the enclosure of our own lives, but with a brave face, we still solider on and continue with our general social dealings, as we see no other options open to us, or we may decide to sacrifice our needs to help others, such as in care and commitment to our loved ones.

- By this stage, our sense of mistrust with many concepts and people may substantially increase through our accumulated personal experiences and disappointments with unworkable current methods and social practices.

- We may feel at a loss and begin to question everything. Some may try different workshops, new studies of human, social sciences or alternative perspectives. Some may be more eagerly committed than others for their individual search for the truth.

7.

How much of children's innate potential is lost through their social conditioning?

This is when we reflect on our life's journey and gauge our true state of happiness and satisfaction. In spite of our apparent successes, many who have deprived their opportunity for expressing their sense of purpose often feel a deep sense of unhappiness, regret and stress with their current life achievements and feel somewhat trapped in their current positions.

The summary of sense of loss we may experience

a. **Lack of sense of purpose:** Basically our social and education systems have taught us how to view our clockwork life and comply with social expectations, understand our social methods to help us survive and meet our physical needs. Basically the main focus is placed on how to feed and create a comfortable space for ourselves rather than follow and meet our Purpose in life- what is this body meant to do/ achieve in this world and for the world?

We are constantly reminded through social advertisers and trend setters how to treat our bodies, make them beautiful, have a big comfortable house and keep our minds busy with trivia and stories about our sensational heroes and celebrities. Live a dream of 'what may be' rather than 'what is'. The real substance and meaning of life is hardly ever discussed by the masses. Trivia sells far more than substance would any day of the year. Our state of happy existence in line with our sense of individual purpose is NEVER regarded as the main point of our existence and focus.

Why have we not been taught the importance of our sense of purpose?

Why is it that we are often left in the dark when it comes to the question of the real meaning of life? To examine why we are not awakened to such questions in our education system, first we need to ask why our leaders have let us down and not informed us as educators:

- Is it due to the ignorance and lack of wisdom of our elders/leaders?
- Is it that our leaders don't know enough and just make up stories and reasons as they go along to give themselves some legitimacy to continue with what they know at the time?
- Is it that we have been systematically exploited to serve a few who control us and deliberately

manufacture our realities to suit, keep us miserable in the dark through misinformation, subjugation and deprivation?

I believe the truth lies somewhere between the above points and readers should decide for themselves what their truth might be.

b. **Loss of 'that initial essence' which we brought with ourselves to this life:** To understand how much of children's original qualities mentioned earlier are lost by the time they reach their state of maturity in life, we shall explore the social impact on these early qualities:

Closer to the experience of oneness	
Children's Original Quality	Mature Adult Quality
At the very early stages of life, children have no real understanding of their <u>sense of self</u>. They can't distinguish between themselves and their environment. They have no idea where they actually begin or end. To them it is just one continuum of life without any differentiation or subdivision of objects around them. The sense of conscious awareness of the concept of 'I' forms a bit later in their lives.	Children's initial open perspectives towards their surroundings narrow through their social education. As adults, we develop a sense of individuality and see ourselves separately from many things in life. We are now programmed to be competitive rather than united with others. We see 'us and them' in a more predefined landscape of our life. This can promote the sense of alienation from our systemic social coexistence with each other.

Honest expression of their feelings	
Children's Original Quality	Mature Adult Quality
They only respond to <u>pleasure and pain</u>. If something engages them and makes them happy they keep doing it and if something makes them unhappy they react and complain about it. They don't play politics or mind games. Without any clichés, they say it 'how it is'.	As children we learn social politics and how to play mind games in order to get what we want or take advantage of the situation by simply pretending. We become more complex and begin to lose our initial transparency of being honest and often project a different image to the world than how we may feel inside.

Life is exciting to them	
Children's Original Quality	Mature Adult Quality
The prospect of <u>life is exciting</u> and full of things they don't know; they feel alive. They have that real <u>spark of life</u> in them. There is a life out there to be discovered. The prospect of life is generally full of things they don't know and want to discover. I am sure many of us can relate to that, especially as we get older and feel that we have lost some of that spark.	As we grow older, we lose our initial spark for excitement. This is not just due to our age; it is mostly due to our experience of setbacks and disappointments. Our disappointments are based on false views and the assumption we were taught as children about the reality of life by our educators. Based on our social training, we create an endless set of expectations upon ourselves in order to live the social picture manufactured in our minds. No wonder so many suffer from anxiety and depressions in today's society.

Simple needs in life	
Children's Original Quality	Mature Adult Quality
They are easily pleased with simple things as they have not entered into the concept of consumerism as yet. By and large; a child even in a most basic environment can be happy.	As we grow older, we seem to develop this never ending sensation for having more in order to get our daily satisfaction fix. We live in a consumerist society. We are conditioned to think of our happiness in terms of having more. The problem is that this endless loop will result in more misery than ultimate happiness.

Stimulations & inquisitiveness	
Children's Original Quality	Mature Adult Quality
They love stimulations & interactions on their own terms and as much as they can manage at the time. They are highly inquisitive to learn. For example, they empty a rubbish bin and become fascinated by what they might find in there which usually ends up in their mouths for a quick taste and validation of usefulness in their lives.	The senses of stimulation and inquisitiveness are great qualities that we need throughout our lives as our long term survival depends on them. However, if our social environment is limited and does not support a sense of spontaneity, creativity and reinvention, we could end up becoming less excited to participate in things and explore things that are not appreciated or much regarded by our society.

Open to possibilities	
Children's Original Quality	Mature Adult Quality
They don't apply limitations upon themselves as they can go right to the edge of a cliff, just to see what is on the other side. Everything is possible.	Initial childlike openness to the sense of discovery can be hampered as the social expectation for conformity increases and leaves little room for anyone to explore new possibilities and reinvention potentials on a continuous basis.

Courageous	
Children's Original Quality	Mature Adult Quality
They don't have our conventional fears about the world around them. They have no fear of making mistakes or doing things outside the normal or social context.	As we grow, we become more fearful and mistrusting of what we used to be comfortable with and daring towards. We begin to buy into what has been suggested to us especially when it is substantiated by our own personal experience. For example, how we may lose our confidence about some of our abilities.

Highly imaginative	
Children's Original Quality	Mature Adult Quality
They are highly imaginative and take pleasure in their creativity. For example, they turn a cardboard box into an imaginary car; they draw amazing shapes that they can relate to. We are free of any biases that narrow our scope of possibilities.	Even though the concept of imagination is generally acknowledged in our social education, it is not imaginatively promoted or enabled by our inhibiting social leaders and their practices that trivialise its importance for our survival as a species. Generally we do not allow ample time for imagination to flourish within us and our larger organisations. In our social culture we act far more than we actually think or imagine. Even though everything humanity ever created has always begun with an initial dream, we are openly discouraged from day dreaming and often corrected by our parents to become practical.

Following no social rules	
Children's Original Quality	Mature Adult Quality
They act naturally as they are not socially conscious as yet. The social rules are not known to them as yet. For example, they can freely do whatever they want to do without worrying about what other people may think. The presence of a king or a queen makes no difference to them in what they are about to do.	As we grow up, we learn that in order to avoid unwanted consequences in our lives, we must not express ourselves too openly and should become more selective who we should share our inner personal experiences of the way we see, think and behave. One could say that we begin to hide the truth from others or at times lie, in order to please everyone and have it both ways.

Trusting	
Children's Original Quality	Mature Adult Quality
They trust most things as they don't have preconceived ideas about anything.	As adults, we are more mistrusting of others and our environment than when we were younger. We progressively evolve from mistrusting a given situation to mistrusting the participants and all related associations with that situation. For example, we often mistrust the whole person rather than mistrusting an aspect of them in a given situation. For example, you may not trust a friend to be left alone with your husband for a period of time, but you may trust her wisdom and sciences. Therefore one cannot declare a person in totality as untrustworthy as we often do in society.

Look up to authority & social role models	
Children's Original Quality	Mature Adult Quality
They respect and look up to their guardians' authority and see them as role models.	As we grow, through personal experiences of constantly being let down by those who have persuaded us and claimed to know and have solutions to our lives challenges. Each individual has his/ her list of defamed authority such as self-serving politicians, manmade heroes and so called wise ones.

In summary, our listed innate human qualities seem to decline as we get older and conditioned with the ways of our social norm. The majority of our initial sense of innocence and purity vanishes and is replaced by fear, anxiety, anger and frustration.

c. **Need for Radical Changes:** We soon realise that our current struggles in life will not change unless something more fundamental changes or if we adopt different approaches in the way we think and operate. This is an important realisation for an individual as it would substantially give him/ her a great opportunity to adopt new life saving flexible attitudes to the concept of change and the reinvention of self, rather than becoming a slave and entrenched into his/ her old stubborn un- workable beliefs.

8.

Bitter and disillusioned
grown up people of the world

Life always has a way of dishing out to us unique and individual experiences. Even though we have similar exposures and conditioning by our educational and social systems, each one of us ends up having unique encounters, challenges and develops differently in life. We may share many common traits through our earlier conditioning, but we also display unique differences in our understanding of social context and environment. One could say we have different journeys and we need to live our own distinctive stories. Disregarding of such differences, the majority of people can't escape the negative by-products and pitfalls of our artificial and unworkable social system.

In general people fall in two major groups. Those who are not questioning types and are primarily preoccupied and focused on their success rather than caring much for the bigger social picture. On the other hand there are those who are more socially sensitive and often become more agitated by the discrepancies and are capable of noticing actual flaws in the social system. Given that we all live under the same broken and fragmented social umbrella, both groups at some stage in their lives become disillusioned with their social situations and question the established social mind sets. However, one group often notices such disillusionment much earlier than the other group. In this chapter we shall explore these two perspectives.

Socially Unconscious & Lured Group

Some of us are more conformist and through the process of growing up develop a trusting vison of authority and believe in what we have been told by official sources to be factual and rarely people with such a mind-set will challenge an established view. In general this group of people often seems to have reasonable to prosperous standards of life by comparison to those who have serious experiences of social hardship, let downs or are generally struggling to maintain a basic standard of life.

The reason for such a correlation between conformist people and people with more prosperous life standards may be due to factors such as accidents of birth and individual disposition or fortune for not encountering hardship in life. As you would appreciate the main ingredient that can compel people to break out of their conformist mode and question the validity of their social system is mainly due to their individual experiences of social hardships and deprivation which forces them to look outside the box for answers.

The conformist group often ends up with what appears to be a socially rewarding life. They tend to acquire some level of wealth, perks or power of various qualities. To be in such a position, on the surface, it looks as if society is on your side and things do pay off if one conforms to the prescribed social rule and manmade dynamics.

Those who experience such rewards often remain on real highs for their social and material achievements and this is totally understandable as our social conditioning about success is very much about how much we actually possess in life or how prestigious our life is compared to others. This is the model of success and how we were all raised to aspire to the notion of 'climbing up the ladder of success'. This illusion lures and captivates many of us for a long time as we see our level of worthiness increase within the context of such a painted social model. However, on close examination, we realise that even though at times it seems that we are having a joyful time, deeply we know all this comes at a cost and also it does not last forever. Our overall thirst for substance and the quality of life that we often hope to achieve never feels totally satisfactory and there is something not quite right with it as if something is always missing from this social picture of happiness, especially as we get older and look at our lives. For the majority of us, there is a sense of indescribable emptiness and this type of feeling is often experienced in spite of our accumulated wealth or power. If we examine this social framework of 'how we should socially live', we may notice the following problems:

- Of course there is absolutely nothing wrong with achieving things in life, especially if they are within the holistic context of sense of community. This is totally in line with our sense of individual purpose and should be regarded as part of our systemic contribution in life.

  However, there is always a psychological and physical price tag for achieving anything we do and what we need to weigh up here is our expected social achievement against such a price tag. For example, if we are socially conditioned to constantly chase financial success and if we follow such a path without any deeper consideration, success may come to us at a serious cost potentially to our personal health, family break ups or acquired bad habits and substance abuse as a way of dealing with our highly stressful existence. These inflictions occur because we were – socially hypnotised to believe such pursuits in life will bring us ultimate happiness. The bitter truth is that if we are not consciously aware of the deeper ramification of our actions, we could end up living our lives as slaves and sacrificing what actually matters to us most to follow some shallow social path that we were conditioned to believe was the right recipe handed to us by our trusted elders or so called wise ones in society.

Strive not to be a success, but rather to be of value.

—Albert Einstein

- In spite of enduring psychological stress to achieve our expected material status, as caring human beings, we most likely would have endured a great level of dissatisfaction and hurt for witnessing and turning a blind eye to those in the world who have nothing and are often systemically brutalised by the very same system that is meant to protect them. Even though many of us become desensitised about the pain and plight of such people, we still at some deeper level, will be registering and get traumatised by unavoidable and senseless suffering around us. This often indicates to us there is something wrong in the social culture we blindly follow. Most of us can't live like kings and queens while people are dying and suffering outside our palaces. We don't like such disparity in our social karma.

The testimony of the greatest humans who have ever lived is that the way to make the most of ourselves is by transcending ourselves. We must learn to move beyond self-centredness to make room within ourselves for others. When you transcend yourself, the fact will be confirmed by the

> quality of your life. We will attain – even
> if only momentarily – a transparency and
> a radiance of being which results from
> living both within and beyond yourself.
> This is the promise and excitement of
> self-understanding.

—Don Richard Risco

Sometimes major events can force some conformist individuals to reconsider other perspectives, for example, if their prosperous circumstances change overnight and they find themselves not supported by the system that they previously believed in. Sometimes such a mental shift occurs when people experience health issues or stress that forces them to see and question the shortfalls in their established way of thinking.

For example, as people get older, they may realise that in spite of all their achievements, they may have missed their true sense of purpose in life and they may begin to regret wasting most of their lives on things that really didn't matter much in the end.

Conscious and socially questioning Group

Those of us who are more inquisitive about the bigger picture of life and like the rest of humanity, have innocently gone through the process of childhood social conditioning may gradually realise as we grow older that something is tragically wrong in the foundation of what we were earlier taught in society.

We may notice there is a great difference between the picture that was painted for us about the world and how it actually is. Such divided views and perspectives often become stronger as we begin to notice a steady increase in our level of dissatisfaction with the way we are currently conducting ourselves as a human race in this so called civilised world. We may notice there are appalling social practices that the majority of people find deeply disturbing and often feel embarrassed by, as a human race.

If we are a thinker, we quickly recognise that our society, both at the local and the global scale, is not really designed or deliberately engineered to truly serve or equitably meet its main stakeholders – humanity. If we look closely at social governing structures, we realise they are totally counter intuitive to what they should be.

It seems that there exist great prospects, potential and ingredients in this world that could easily be used to shape the emergence of a great civilisation, but somehow they don't systemically work together and nothing seems to add up the way it should. For every great step forward, many unexpected obstacles emerge and derail the progress, as if there are inbuilt destructive mechanisms deliberately embedded in every corner we look. It feels like these obstacles are there purely to ensure society cannot optimally function, and in the majority of cases the system seems to be working against itself. There is an evil shadowy force always present to ensure we never live as a civilised race in total peace and harmony.

In spite of the best desires of almost the entire human race, we still have poverty/ wars/ violation of human rights, avoidable diseases and environmental disasters. Somehow there seems to be an unpredictable and strange volatility in the psyche of our planet.

Socially conscious people become disillusioned with their social rules much earlier than the conformist group. Many will continue to seek solutions in alternative philosophical, esoteric and scientific literature. This group truly represents the hope for the future of humanity as any potential change to our broken social structure is only possible if enough people recognise social pitfalls in the first place.

9.

Why our world is the way it is – Cruel and Ignorant?

In this chapter, we investigate the fundamental reasons why we need to change and explore what is actually wrong with our society and practices.

This is a very serious and important topic for us to discover and if we don't truly appreciate what is actually wrong with our current social system, there will be no hope for any potential future social improvements.

This discovery is intended to be stimulating and will give your intelligent mind an opportunity to grapple with real issues in the world, allow you to logically examine what works and why. Finally help you to visualise how we can intelligently devise plans and change our destiny as a human race.

As much as I would like to present to you motivational and inspirational messages in this book for how we can reshape our world for the better, unfortunately, in this chapter, we need to focus on what is actually wrong with our world. It is a great struggle for me to stay inspirational while my topic reveals the most horrific and unfair cruelties that are currently taking place around the world.

So, on that note, please put up with me for being too explicit in the following chapter as I have no option, but to say it how it is in order to do justice to the reality of our world.

An upfront warning, the topic of current world issues is a serious one and unless you are totally interested in how we are currently positioned within society and shaped by various elements in the world, you may find it too confronting or unsettling.

However, in my view as more people understand and recognise the current pitfalls in our civilisation, the easier it will be for humanity at large to collectively change its destiny.

> Our lives begin to end the day we become silent about things that matter.
> **—Martin Luther King Jr.**

The Root Causes of Our Systemic Social failings

Before we can seriously rectify the obvious pitfalls in the fabric of our social mind-sets and practices, the ones that are glaringly lacking in essential substance and foundation to intelligently support humanity in an equitable and sustainable way, we need to ask the following questions.

Are these systemic social shortfalls due to a deliberate and conscious intention by the social regulators to manipulate and rob humanity of its legitimate rights or are these shortfalls due to innocent ignorance, lack of essential know how or capability by our leaders past and present? The following section examines certain facts to answer these questions.

To simply understand what is wrong with our current civilisation just turn on your TV and watch the news. It is truly disgraceful to witness humanity acting so shamefully and wilfully allowing the whole fabric of our civilisation to collapse so mercilessly. This seriously brings to question why we live in such a cruel and ignorant world. Is it through our conscious and collective choice or are we clandestinely coerced by our social designers to live as such?

We need to understand why, as so called civilised people, we seem to be living in a totally uncivilised world, and with all our technological advancements we still have unworkable frameworks and practices. Who is behind all this and why are many innocent people, through no fault of their own, are often systemically abused, brutalised and displaced.

In order for you to appreciate and get some understanding of the magnitude of our global social demise, I would like to ask you to get in touch with your heart and see the victimised people of the world. If you truly believe in the concept of humanity, you will also begin to feel deeply for these innocent discarded people, who are just like you or me and in essence, they are our forgotten brothers and sisters. They are often being totally ignored and discounted by the social and justice system in this world.

These people are not statistics or numbers that can

easily be dismissed. They are not unfortunate species of a different type on the other side of the planet that don't matter much to anyone. As a civilised society we need to regard every soul on this Earth as the essence of divinity and realise they greatly matter to humanity. Every human life is worth preserving and every person is worthy of being honoured, loved and respected.

Why and how have we collectively forgotten these basic innate and caring qualities that make us human? Why do we live in constant fear and in our own little petty segregated islands? What happened to our deep human loving connections that make us feel alive and give us a reason to live harmoniously and mutually interact with one another?

If we call ourselves civilised human beings, then whatever happens anywhere in this world, without any doubt, will systemically impact and involve us all. It is not somebody else's issues but ours to resolve.

Right now, our humanity is at a crucial cross road. The current social and systemic failures have compounded to a very serious and explosive situation. To understand how we have failed so badly as a race for letting our world slide down this far, we need to look at some facts and it does not matter how we cut it, we cannot escape from the obvious systemic cruelties that are persistently failing our humanity.

It has actually passed the point where some ignorant prejudice views labelling or ridiculing those who speak out about injustices of this world as cheap sensationalists or delusional conspiracy theorists. Such dismissive views do not wash anymore. There is absolutely no misunderstanding here and there is no distortion or fabrication of the truth. Facts speak for themselves. It is clear for all to see that our world social structure or our official systems have failed to let us live in peace, and have prevented us from thriving and excelling as the divine and creative beings that we truly are.

> In our age there is no such thing as 'keeping out of politics'. All issues are political issues, and politics itself is a mass of lies, evasions, folly, hatred and schizophrenia.
>
> **—George Orwell**

We just cannot look the other way and escape from the truth anymore. What truth you may ask? The truth that on one side of the equation, we have the following points to consider:

Fact 1 – Mass Human Fatality

Thousands of innocent people are unnecessarily dying every single day. That is a fact. They are dying through malnutrition, wars and avoidable diseases. I know it may not be too alarming to some of you as you might be used to such reoccurring daily events. Unfortunately we have become so accustomed to these abhorrent acts of cruelty and murder that news of a mass murder which we might hear today is nothing out of the ordinary to us anymore. Is it? Why, because there were some mass murders yesterday and the day before and so on.

Of course none of us like to witness human cruelty, but unfortunately we are so used to having it around and involuntarily we have accepted it as part of our normal lives and part of our so called civilised existence. The only wish we have is that such nastiness does not happen to us or to our loved ones; otherwise, we just accept it as our normal way of living and as our human fate.

I am sorry to remind us that this is not our human fate, this is certainly not who we are and this is not how it should be. We have been made to believe that human nature is cruel and violent. Unfortunately we ended up accepting such distorted views as our realities. The reason for such deliberate social conditioning will become more obvious as we journey through this book.

> So much of what we are currently seeing as far as human suffering and misery comes from diseases that should have been preventable but were not.
>
> **—Francis Collins**

Fact 2 – Displaced and Homeless People

Millions of people, through no fault of their own are homeless. They have no sanitation, no safe drinking water that we may take for granted every day. Many are just barely alive, sleeping under the stars or if they are lucky, they may live in some ungodly shanty towns trying very hard to restore some sense of dignity and honour as a human being.

Most of them sleep with an empty stomach and watch helplessly the demise of their children and families day in and day out. It is sad to say that every official international effort or response to such human tragedies, at best, has focused on dealing with the symptoms. It is absolutely guaranteed. So they send aid and provide assistance to deal with the symptoms but there is never a coordinated official response or action that focusses on addressing and **eradicating** the root causes of the impending problems. Why is that?

What is failing here is that no one is seriously tackling the actual system, that by design, generated human suffering in the first place and unless the system changes, the human misery will continue unabated.

All the aid agencies such as Red Cross, which of course always do a great job, no question about that, can never address the root causes of the systemic failures which resulted in such chaos in the first place. They just provide simple band aids to the needy and the root cause of the systemic miseries will remain untouched. So what do you think is actually stopping the official international community from addressing the root causes, the system that by deliberate design pumps out suffering on a daily basis? Think about it. Is it because the international community doesn't have the necessary intelligence to deal with the problems or is it because nobody dares to touch or alter the system that by design creates such suffering?

By the way, which official international body do you think is actually responsible for addressing and <u>illuminating</u> the root causes of human misery in our world? I'll let you think about that.

> We have come dangerously close to accepting the homeless situation as a problem that we just can't solve.
>
> **—Linda Lingle**

Fact 3 – Large Scale Fear for Survival

Millions live in a constant state of fear every single day. Fear for their survival, for being unfairly arrested, incarcerated or victimised. They just don't know who will arrive on their doorstep in the middle of the night and snatch their loved ones, brutalise them and take their possessions away.

There is no system of justice for them. There is nowhere for them to run to. There is no responsible authority to complain to and let's face it, officially we in the west hear some sympathetic noises through our media, but unofficially nobody really gives a dam about their plight or the violation of their human rights. Do they? Because if the official international bodies did give a dam, we wouldn't be having such a sustained level of suffering today. Would we? It would have been eradicated many decades ago.

> If everyone howled at every injustice, every
> act of barbarism, every act of unkindness,
> then we would be taking the first step
> towards a real humanity.
>
> **—Nelson DeMille**

Fact 4 – Lack of Education

Millions miss out on decent education and are never given essential social nurturing. Due to such obvious social neglect they can never demonstrate their individual potential and capabilities.

These poor people are not given a chance to rise and shine as a human being and experience a sense of worthiness about themselves, or the possibility of effectively and positively contributing to society and feeling good about their self-worth.

> A human being is not attaining his full
> heights until he/ she is educated.
>
> **—Horace Mann**

They never get the opportunity to feel socially loved or cared for as they are generally and conveniently abandoned by the system. Our animals in the well to do world often receive more love and care than some of these innocent forgotten people. Don't you agree?

Just look at your Facebook and see how animals are pampered and regarded by so many People. Of course animals should be loved unconditionally, and so should the forgotten innocent people of the world. Think of the plight of the helpless boys & girls, young children and elderly who are in essence our conveniently abandoned brothers and sisters.

Please close your eyes for a moment and truly walk in their shoes – that is if they have any shoes. Become totally voiceless, powerless, unloved, abandoned and lonely. How does it feel to be totally rejected by society? Honestly doesn't this make you feel like crying in your heart and soul? How can we, the civilised people ignorantly live in a blatant vacuum and be blasé about our shameful world? It is truly tragic.

There is a hell of lot wrong in the social picture I have just painted for you, but remember every inhumane situation that I mentioned here, without question is totally avoidable. Doesn't this make you feel angry? Doesn't this make you wonder why the world is the way it is and why such unnecessary misery has to go on unquestioned by those who are supposed to be responsible for our welfare?

What we can intelligently deduce here is that all our exploitations have systemically and intentionally been designed and manufactured in order to keep people in a constant state of misery. To some of you these statements may appear a bit farfetched and unreal. For this reason please stay with facts rather than with your emotions. I truly wish I was wrong here, but unfortunately we can't close our eyes and ignore what is in front of us any longer. We are human beings and surely the meaning of humanity must have some significance for us. Just look at the futile misery around us and seriously question why it is so.

So far I have explained certain facts about the current level of human suffering, now, let's look at the other side of the equation and talk about other interesting facts.

Fact 5 – Disproportional Global Wealth Distribution

Without question or shadow of doubt, we know there are a handful of individuals in this world who possess almost the entire global wealth. We are referring to an obscene amount of power and this is not an exaggeration. It is truly unimaginable the size and the amount of wealth they actually possess. Such wealth is the result of an unfair and inequitable accumulation of money over centuries by a few influential member of the privileged class. Sometimes they are referred to as the Elite class, Oligarchy, Illuminati or Cabal. My statements are not about witch hunt for any particular group and for this, I shall refer to such privileged groups with a new label of – **the Self-Serving class.**

> For far too long the world's poorest people have seen no benefit from the vast natural resources in their own backyards. It is time to end the injustice where ordinary people are silent witnesses, left to suffer without basic services, as the profits from their countries' assets are hidden and plundered by corrupt regimes.
>
> **—Nick Clegg**

Did you know that the majority of the Earth's wealth is received by the same nameless top one percent and the rest of the population receive leftover specks and crumbs, that is if they we are lucky? Because we know for a fact that a great majority of innocent people are left out of the prosperity equation and with no real prospect of respite anytime soon, they often unfairly struggle and many die through social neglect and physical hunger. Their death is of little or no consequence to the rest of the well to do world of the privileged class.

> The last study on income distribution in USA showed us that 93% of all new income created went to the top 1% while the bottom 99% of the population enjoyed the remaining 7%. When we are talking about Oligarchy form of government, it is not just a handful of families owning the entire nation, we are also talking about owning the political life of the nation.
> **—Senator Bernie Sanders (presidential candidate 2016)**

Does this surprise you? Well there is nothing new here as this has been going on for many generations. The privileged class have always been invisibly ruling the world from a distance. They are not answerable to any governments. Their wealth and power are outside governmental jurisdiction and control. Almost as if they belong to another planet with different rules and immunities.

We all understand that amongst other things, governments are there to establish and uphold equitable and just laws to ensure a fair distribution of wealth amongst their citizens. Of course that is an important job for any responsible elected government. If this is true then, it really makes you wonder what elaborate system of manipulation must be in place that even the governments have no say in how wealth is distributed. Sometimes governments, which are generally made up of ordinary people, are also victims of these supreme powers.

For example, when poor American or Australian governments are in debt by billions if not trillions of dollars, then who are they in debt to? Where does such a vast amount of collected interest go? Does this incredible amount of wealth ever see daylight by normal people of the world? Obviously Not. We know many are dying of hunger every day when our collective earthly wealth is too unimaginable for most people to comprehend.

Who actually own such powerful private institutions and where did the money that was issued to the governments came from in the first place? Our international, governmental and social systems are often deliberately manipulated at their essential cores by certain invisible and highly influential people. They are invisible because we never publicly hear from these people.

As a result, the social and governmental systems which are meant to serve their precious members (humanity) become totally dysfunctional and keep on failing to equitably and fairly meet basic human, social and environmental needs.

> It is economic power that determines political power, and governments become the political functionaries of economic power.
>
> **—Jose Saramago**

Think about it? Why do we have so much unjustified suffering and why are there so many disadvantaged, poor and hungry people in this world? Why do we still have human slavery/ child labour/ child soldiers, helpless communities living in abject poverty and wars that none of us want?

Fact 6 – Deliberate Large Scale World Imbalances & Demise

You don't have to be a genius or a social architect to work out the devastating effect of such global scale imbalances on humanity. You can work it out for yourself and appreciate the generated negative human psyche and physical magnitude of the pain which has been directed on ordinary and innocent people.

From the social coherence and systemic health perspective of the planet, this is a tragic recipe for disasters of significant proportions. The causal effect of such injustices will tear the world apart and this is more or less what we are currently witnessing when we look at the news and observe the scale of human devastation.

> There is a need for financial reform along ethical lines that would produce in its turn an economic reform to benefit everyone. This would nevertheless require a courageous change of attitude on the part of political leaders.
>
> **—Pope Francis**

Due to these self-inflicted systemic imbalances, world events have become very predictable. The current state of our social demise is almost scientifically calculable. It is basically the symptoms or the by-products of our created world of cause and effect.

There are absolutely no justifications for creating such a great disparity amongst humanity and deliberately destabilising the foundations of our social structure all in the name of power and wealth for a few.

> There can be no peace in the world so long as a large proportion of the population lack the necessities of life and believe that a change of the political and economic system will make them available. World peace must be based on world plenty.
>
> **—John Boyd Orr**

Fact 7 – War Money Making Machines

Let's not kid ourselves: conflicts and wars are highly profitable. For some, wars are the greatest avenue to untold riches. There is no business like the war business to quickly generate an incredible amount of wealth. Why? Because wars give the Self-Serving ones a great opportunity to globally sell arms of all sizes and shapes to the order of trillions of dollars.

They can sell to anyone who wishes to buy them and once these created wars have turned towns and cities into rubble, of course another great opportunity immediately becomes possible and that is to rebuild what was destroyed at an extortionate cost, potentially many times more than their original worth.

This means the ones who have lost absolutely everything in such devastating conflicts, now have to borrow money from the international monetary institutions owned by the privileged class to pay for the reconstruction of what was taken away from them and the world of human abuse and suffering will go round and round as it always has.

> Political language is designed to make lies sound truthful and murder respectable, and to give an appearance of solidity to pure wind.
>
> **–George Orwell**

For as long as anyone can remember, there have always been wars and conflicts. Why, because it generates an incredible amount of wealth and opportunity for certain minorities.

For example, during the World Wars and other conflicts since, many profited incredibly well by supporting both sides of the conflicts and hedging their bets evenly. For those of you interested in history, there is plenty of alternative material you can read, research and learn about what actually took place in these conflicts and how little the public knew about what actually went on.

We should also not forget the devastating and tragic consequences of war on innocent human populations. Of course to those cruel minorities, this is of no great consequence as they have no respect for human lives. They think of innocent people as 'human cattle', simple and gullible and if they kill some people today, there will be plenty more born tomorrow to replace them.

In any case, the cruel ones don't like an over populated world as it would crowd their style, so for them it is not necessarily a bad idea to prune humanity with a few nudges and in the process make some decent money. Basically why not kill two birds with one stone. How clever is that. Refer to the 'World Order' manifesto on depopulation.

So it appears creating wealth is quite easy for the money thirsty ones, but there is a big catch here, these ruthless beings can't just openly start a new war as that would be just too obvious and could unnecessarily raise people's suspicions about their evil intent.

Therefore, they need to find the right excuse before they can kick start any new wars. So they create disguises, diversions and psychological lies to create unimaginable staged mayhem or sensationally charged social situations in order to grab people's attention, guide people's opinion in their desired direction and create an opportunity to convince the masses of the legitimacy of their impending inhumane actions. So they begin to create fictional scenarios, hypnotise the masses through official media and turn people against one another so the money making machine just keeps rolling.

> We live in a society in which spurious realities are manufactured by the media, by governments, by big corporations, by religious groups, political groups. I ask, in my writing, 'What is real?' Because unceasingly we are bombarded with pseudo realities manufactured by very sophisticated people using very sophisticated electronic mechanisms.
> **—Philip K. Dick**

Fact 8 – Blaming the Innocents

The ordinary people are often portrayed as the evil masterminds behind the current atrocities around the world. They are generally used as scapegoats and falsely blamed/ categorised by the ruling class as cruel, greedy and war mongers. This is obviously far from the truth. By and large, the true nature of human beings is kind, caring and bubbles with empathy for one another. You can always witness this in times of major crisis when everybody genuinely and generously pulls together, hand in hand, to help a fellow man in need. For example, bush fires, Earth quakes or flooding always bring out and demonstrate the human caring nature operating at its peak.

I also acknowledge that in some rare or infrequent situations we (the ordinary people) have the potential to behave badly and conduct regretful acts outside our general good nature such as petty crimes of passion, rape, stealing or physical harm to others. I believe the majority of such behaviour is due to our social/systemic factors and failures rather than due to any innate or inherent factors relating to the nature of our human make up (it is nurture rather than nature). The conditions that can invoke uncharacteristic human behaviour are such things as:

1. A bitter or misguided individual upbringing which can often be attributed to a bad social, educational or environmental condition. The external social factors are generally responsible as they systemically contribute to such inhumane reactions.

2. Deprivation of basic human needs which again is very much the result of the systemic social failure that could influence and guide the reaction to a situation.

3. Deliberate psychological manipulation of an individual to commit crimes. This again is a

powerful psychological tool commonly used by many to effectively turn people against one another. This is often intended to destabilise the social system for specific clandestine gains.

4. When an individual's life or their loved ones are threatened, or when an individual feels somehow cornered/under threat and needs to defend him/ herself.

However, I don't believe, not for one moment that ordinary people are capable of performing systemic terror on a mass scale such as what is currently and mercilessly sweeping the world right now.

It feels somewhat alien and totally unreal for most ordinary people to fathom how a very small number of individuals could become so incredibly powerful, manipulative and barbaric that with some form of blanket immunity and cleaver disguises can system-ically, ruthlessly and with great precision conduct terror against the rest of humanity and get away with it. The irony is that they can openly conduct the most amazing acts of cruelty and at the same time, point fingers at ordinary people who generally wish to survive and be left in peace. Just ask all the moms and dads of this world what they think of wars.

Al Qaeda was deliberately created, trained and supported by the US government.

—Senator Hillary Clinton (presidential candidate 2016)

Due to the good nature of innocent and law abiding citizens, the Self-Serving class subtle mind control techniques are often not noticeable as people can't believe such systemic evil could possibly be operating here so they continue to live in an innocent world where everything is done with the best of intentions, integrity and in the name of justice, especially if it is endorsed by higher social orders and authorities.

We must always acknowledge that ordinary people in general are innocent and it makes no difference whether you are a decent board member, a CEO or a hardworking clark, whether you work for government agencies, NGOs, private organisations or media. Devious and manipulative strategies are often conjured up at a much higher level so it is almost invisible for most ordinary people to notice. All we can witness is the aftermath of such devastating strategies resulting in chaos, cruelty and human deprivation.

Ask anybody you know, friends, family or colleagues, if they would subscribe to wars, practice cruelty or allow injustices to take place in their lives? Ask them if they would welcome a war in their immediate neighbourhood and if they are prepared to expect tanks and soldiers marching up and down their streets, killing people and destroying their properties and livelihoods.

It will be very surprising if anybody in your life would subscribe to such inhumanity. Think about it; if it is not people you personally know in your life, then who actually sponsors such insane inhumanity?

If average moms and dads genuinely want peace and harmony for themselves and their families, then who on earth sponsor wars and terrorises the world in our names?

> To prefer evil to good is not in human nature; and when a man is compelled to choose one of two evils, no one will choose the greater when he might have the less.
>
> **—Plato**

When you think about it, for those of us who can see through such an engineered web of deceit, it is almost comical, how such a minority group easily get away with major crimes, but of course it is not funny at all for those who are at the receiving end. Such clever strategies and tactics appear so far-fetched that many of us who believe in human decency can't possibly comprehend that such systemic manipulation could possibly go on unnoticed. But if you consciously look for clues and facts, sometimes outside your mainstream official media, they are right there and they are pretty much in black and white.

Fact 9 – Legitimising Arms Sales through Manufactured Wars

The statements I have made so far are definitely not created from my imagination. They are not hearsay or old wives tales. As we know for sure, many people are suffering in cruel and devastating ways every single day, while global arms production is expanding at an alarming rate and already has established its presence as a legitimate worldwide industry, with international trade fairs showing off their latest arsenals, just as if they are selling white goods to the public or lollies to kids.

Never forget the very basic aim of a military weapon is not for innocent target practice; it is especially designed to kill, or maim human beings and destroy their livelihoods as effectively as possible until nothing is standing upright. It is pretty disgusting just to think about it, especially in the context of our current level of humanity in the 21st century. For heaven sake we are so smart that we can land a space craft on a fast moving comet in deep space, yet our leaders choose to endorse and allow the manufacture of the most ungodly and devastating weapons humanity has ever known. There is something fundamentally repulsive in such inexcusable inhumanity.

The lucrative weapons industry can't survive unless people need weapons and are required to use them on a frequent basis, otherwise there will be no viable arms industry or a potential market. Therefore in order to provide incentives and reasons for people to use weapons, we need a forum and it is called man-ufactured or staged wars, where anybody can legiti-mately kill the next person and totally get away from being socially labelled a murderer.

Everybody's worried about stopping
terrorism. Well, there's a really easy way:
stop participating in it.

—Noam Chomsky

The cruel ones can't afford to waste precious time, so they constantly conjure up new wars of choice, make serious money and create mass human tragedies, all in the name of justice. They disguise that goodies are legitimately fighting the baddies. But the truth is that both sides of the conflict are often supported by the same faceless shadowy people who are simply trying to make some opportunities for themselves.

I know it all sounds pretty horrific, but at least we have established there is a big shadowy world of manipulation out there that constantly and intentionally generates misery for the majority of innocent people and if left alone, it will continue with business as usual with even more elaborate disguises and greater infliction of pain on the innocents.

So enough of negativities, it is actually quite draining, even for me just writing about these nightmares that are currently facing humanity. But at least we have identified and established our baseline here. Now we know where we stand and what dynamics are governing us. We can now understand why our entire social system has been deliberately manipulated at the root in order to control and guide humanity down the current world of chaos.

10.

How should we view our Social position & potential?

In this chapter, we shall discuss what our human and social rights are and how we can prepare ourselves for the possibility of a significant social change through our collective human imagination and power.

A dream world of existence

Imagine a world where there are no wars or conflicts. A sustainable green world where there is equitability and plenty for all to share and enjoy. Envisage the world as a tolerant place where no one bothers you for what you are practicing or what you are passionate about. No one will persecute you for your personal beliefs or views. Imagine a great and nurturing society that consciously promotes social values and human freedom. Imagine a society which by design allows you to explore arts and sciences as you please. Imagine a social structure that allows you to live a fulfilling life and supports you in your systemic endeavours and contributions.

What are our legitimate human/ social rights and how to use them

I believe a new era for human empowerment is here and we as a deserving human race can consciously change what we don't believe is honourably or holistically serving us and directly influence how we would like to live going forward.

Historically it has been said the only time a social revolution becomes possible is when at least 51 percent of the population becomes educated. This refers to the essential critical mass required for tipping the balance in favour of social justice and rise in social standards. This means when people's conscious awareness rises to a sufficient level, they begin to understand the truth about their plight and they can no longer tolerate living as a subservient underclass.

> The paradox of education is precisely this – that as one begins to become conscious one begins to examine the society in which he is being educated.
>
> **—James A. Baldwin**

It is also said that the oppressing ruling class is fully aware of the potential for such dire implications and for this reason they ensure that educational evolution does not organically arise in society. So it is in their best interest to keep people educationally as under developed as possible and in elaborate ways confuse them with a barrage of misinformation and guided psychological suggestions. However, with the recent invention of internet and the power of social media, such social manipulation is gradually proving harder to manage effectively than ever before. So for this reason the privacy laws internationally have been systemically violated so everything we individually believe or think instantly becomes the property of the state to judge as friendly or adversary.

> The whole educational and professional training system is a very elaborate filter, which just weeds out people who are too independent, and who think for themselves, and who don't know how to be submissive, and so on — because they're dysfunctional to the institutions.
>
> **—Noam Chomsky**

Our so called governing leaders who never disappoint us with our low expectations of them, continue to consistently and blatantly fail us every time we elect them into power. They are either ethically corrupt or just ignorant which in either case they should not have the legitimacy to be in charge of their current positions and keep continuing to rule us like a bunch of gullible subspecies that don't know or deserve any better and are not worthy of entitlement for decent human rights.

We as a human race should not tolerate political games, mass media manipulations and deliberate inaction by our leaders while the innocent people are being unfairly treated and subjected to continuous unnecessary suffering and worst, may even die in our so called civilised world. This is not acceptable and should no longer be tolerated by deserving and decent human beings.

Most ordinary people witness suffering on a daily basis and consequently feel a sense of internal anger and a lump in their throat, as they witness unnecessary and senseless human misery. As a human race we often feel shameful living in such a cruel world. Especially when we all know, it is quite possible for us to live in a much more humane and nurturing world. Perhaps we have not learnt how to reject the way we have been treated and don't know how to peacefully and collectively stand for what we believe in.

Recognise your potential and exercise your rights

As human beings, deep down, we know that we are truly smart and we have proven our intelligence over thousands of years of human evolution. We demonstrated that through our direct intention and desire we can achieve anything we want. We sent a man to the moon decades ago, yet somehow and very mysteriously our leaders keep on failing to create a harmonious society in which all of us can holistically prosper through systemic coherence and mutual collaboration with one another. I don't believe we should accept any more excuses why we can't live in a civilised world.

The real solution cannot be about uprising against the state or getting into a fight with oppressors and manipulators. <u>Definitely NOT</u> as this type of attitude is exactly what the barbarians thrive on –'wars and destructions' and we, the ordinary people can't possibly become callous and act barbarically like them. I am simply saying that we need to consciously become more aware that:

1. Currently, we truly reside in an unspoken, almost invisible social cage which we are conditioned to accept and subscribe to and call it 'our lives'. In this cage some of us get fed crumbs, the illusion of self-determination and the concept of imaginary freedom;

2. As long as we are within the cage boundaries and don't question why there is a small group of influential individuals with unimaginable perks and powers outside the cage roaming freely, we may be left alone, given permission to continue living our lives as slaves. We may even be rewarded with extra crumbs as an incentive for conforming to their prescribed world and following their double standard ways;

3. The cage can immediately disappear if we choose to realise that we, the people are a far greater species, more powerful and intelligent than those who are unfairly managing us and keeping us captive within their woven paradigm and social definitions.

As some would say, we are similar to a lion that was told he was a sheep and he bought such a suggestion on trust. Therefore for a long time the lion lived and acted like a sheep because he was told to. He was reduced to a demeaning and compromised life of suffering. He tolerated and accepted his fate and continued to live in an artificial shadowy reality. Finally through conscious realisation and observation, he became awakened and recognised that he was a majestic lion with a great spirit and there was no cage big enough to confine him or his amazing abilities. Then he instantly became totally free and took charge of his own destiny. He did not have to fight his oppressors, he just had to realise who he really was and his captors virtually disappeared into thin air.

> Remember no one can make you feel inferior without your consent.
> **—Eleanor Roosevelt**

So for our own sake, we need to become awakened as quickly as we can, step out of the cage and realise that we really don't need to be constantly back peddling and trying to justify our legitimacy for existence. We no longer need to argue our way for what is rightfully ours to start with. We simply need to demand and claim them openly with confidence. For example, we can vote those who don't serve us caringly, honourably and equitably out of office. We should do it intelligently rather than getting into direct conflict with anyone. We can use our so called democratic powers to confidently shape our world the way we want. If we chose to, we can recreate a world of peace and harmony to collectively enjoy and prosper.

11.

Understanding our inner forces prior to embarking on changing the bigger world?

How do we create a civilised and nurturing social structure that can wisely support and nurture our precious people? Can we really create a social system that can intelligently, equitably and sustainably serve us to live a fulfilling and purposeful life?

Can such a social system holistically educate our children with real life substance to help them excel in their unlimited potential? Is the notion of an intelligent social model and practice out of the realm of reality or an impossible dream, especially in view of our current supressed world of instability, turmoil and unjustified human suffering? As a human race do we have the required critical mass, strong will and capability to create such reality for ourselves?

I believe collectively we have great imagination and capabilities to make the necessary inroads to a desired new society. In order to start the process of social healing and reinventing a new civilised world, first we need to do some personal soul searching, answer some fundamental questions about ourselves as a human race and change ourselves intelligently for the better.

> Yesterday I was clever, so I wanted to change the world. Today I am wise so I am changing myself.
>
> **—Rumi**

We need to **search in deep places** and source philosophies, scientific principles and templates that are based on the **true essence of human make up** and its true social needs. We then need **to question and redesign our original programming** in the way we individually 'think and behave' before we can create our sustainable social structures.

> An unexamined life is not worth living.
>
> **—Socrates**

The following sections are worthy of considerations as they have great potential for challenging us to look deeper for real answers and possibilities.

Human Potential & Possibilities

According to our leading scientific theories about the nature of reality, "all life potential and possibilities exist and are accessible at the same time to all of us". In other words, everything is possible if we see it that way. This interesting proposition directly leads us to the following questions:

- Why and how have we individually ended up with our current particular possibilities and experiences in life?
- How and why did we choose such options and possibilities?
- If we don't like our current situations, how come we selected them in the first place and continue to live with them in spite of our conscious dissatisfaction?
- If we didn't select these particular life possibilities and don't even like them, then who selected them and why?

There are no black and white answers to these tantalising questions. However, what is interesting is that at least intelligently we know if we realise that our current position is not adequate or not serving us well we should be able to consciously adopt new ways of thinking and through such a foundation, bring about improved positions and experiences for ourselves. What Quantum Mechanics tells us is that all positions and possibilities exist simultaneously for us right now, but somehow, sometimes we fail to believe in them or acknowledge their potential to manifest, therefore we don't even see or mentally gravitate towards them, so on that basis, they are never likely to become our reality with such a self-fulfilling negative mind set. So the strength of our individual beliefs can take us a long way towards our wants and desires.

I would like to highlight here that once we stop separating and dividing our comprehension of all that is in existence into separate parts (i.e. to lose our concept of self-identity and merge ourselves into 'what is'), then, it is possible for us to begin to see all possibilities as one continuum of just <u>being</u> and in that context, like a magician, reform our current perceptions of self to other compositions and possibilities (re-emergence).

Doorway of possibilities – The reason we often fail to reach and experience the ever present ultimate life realities is not due to our lack of perceived physical tools or methodologies available to us at a given time. It is our lack of profound realisation of our internal essence and our dormant conscious awareness for simply acknowledging life for what it actually is and how it relates to us at every moment. Our limited personal perceptions of reality about our world and the nature of our systemic interactions, result in our doorway of possibilities to close over more and more as we travel through life.

Our perception about reality in the main is a subjective phenomenon and in relation to the ultimate truth, one can never be sure of the authenticity of one's derived internal views and experiences of what is around.

> If we can entertain the possibility that everything "we believe in", "know of" and "act upon" could be totally or partially flawed, then we can begin to open to the possibility for direct experiences with the world around us.
>
> **—Hamid Soltani**

We can bypass our gatekeeper – the subjective reality lens of the subconscious and allow ourselves to see clearly and have memorable experiences. This unreliability of our internally manufactured views does not imply that we should promote the concept of self-doubt or adopt a pessimistic/ untrustworthy attitude to self and life. The concept here is about self-awakening and deliberate adoption of new experiences and possibilities.

Challenges for entering the Door Way – This journey will demand the seeker's genuine love and interest in exploring new possibilities to help them experience the presence of their true conscious state of being. This journey also requires the right level of spiritual readiness for trusting and building enough courage in the inquirer so that it allows him/ her to take a leap through the uncharted world of conscious existence. Of course, the challenge for all of us is how to manage our subconscious mind which is always present and ready to derail any new spark of consciousness experience and consideration of possibilities for change. The subconscious can trivialise the whole idea, confuse the conscious with doubts, divide views and force the inquirer to abandon his/ her plan and force them to retreat back to the old ways of pleasing the current subconscious beliefs. I shall discuss in details the role of the subconscious mind in the next chapter.

Who are we – the Concept of 'I'?

We often refer to ourselves as 'I'. What does that really mean? Who exactly do we refer to when we say 'I am tired or I want this or I can't do that'?

Simon King

What does that 'I' represent?

You can never be sure where exactly this 'I' is within you, especially if you have your eyes closed and deprive yourself of visual stimulation, but somehow you know it exists. There is something that we call 'I' and it seems to exist somewhere within the confinement of the body.

The 'I' experiences life through the use of its body's capabilities on offer. That is the purpose of the body (it is there to serve the master) the 'I'. The Body is the 'I's' vehicle so the 'I' can implement things and achieve things to please the 'I'. The body's ultimate contribution to the 'I' is in serving the 'I's' needs for its external engagement such as the use of hands, arms and legs to interact with the world. In exchange, the body (the servant) gets fed and taken care of by the intelligence of the 'I' that knows how to obtain resources for the body. As a matter of fact, all the amazing objects that we see around us and often take for granted in life such as buildings, vehicles, computers, aeroplanes, etc. have been created by human hands and the legs that allowed them the mobility they needed to conduct their interactions with their environment.

So we interact with the world through our limbs and our limbs also need to be properly sustained and looked after so they can function properly day after day for us. That is why our body's trunk is designed to process food so our internal cells, organs and limbs can be nourished once the 'I' can order the hands to bring the food to the mouth of the body. Our body has its own intelligence for maintaining itself as long as it receives what it needs to function. The body's intelligence far exceeds the intelligence of what we refer to as 'I'. For example, our internal organs are elegantly structured and function intelligently without our direct conscious awareness. We have very little idea of the body/ machine we are occupying. As individuals, we have absolutely no idea how to communicate or control our organs such as liver, kidney or heart. Our liver performs the most amazing functions that are so alien to our conscious level of understanding. Even with our amazing scientific know how and technological advancements, there is no way we can replicate the function of our liver in a laboratory setting.

The simple deduction here is that – we certainly did not design or create our bodies, we have no idea how the body works internally. We just use it and of course, feed it as required so it can keep on serving us with its presence. It is possible to conclude that 'I' is totally different to the body it occupies. This is similar to the concept of a driver being a different entity to the car it drives.

Imagine the sense of 'I' as the driver of this amazing machine called body. Every morning when you wake up (that 'I', wakes up), you (the 'I' energy) find yourself placed in the driving seat with keys in your hand and you begin to use the joystick and operate this machine until you go back to bed and lose your wakefulness. Every morning you drive your body/ the machine, you command it to twist and turn in order to pick up a jar from the cupboard. You take the body to shops, direct your biological mechanical arms to pick up things and then place what you have picked in the shopping trolley. By now the body's mechanical legs (the wheels) have travelled many kilometres and it is getting dark, so you decide to go home to rest so you go to your bedroom (the garage) to park your body, wash it, change its oil in the bath room, feed and rest the body in bed. Don't forget this garage (your home) has a warm bed with a flat screen TV on the wall. It is clean so the machine, your body, can rest and be ready for another day of action in the morning.

> You don't have a soul. You are a soul.
> You have a body.
>
> **—C.S. Lewis**

So where should we start exploring this 'I'?
Let's start from the beginning and slowly peel off this multi-layered puzzle with care, fascination and patience.

Exercise
You could do this exercise if you wish – just stand in front of your favourite mirror and only focus on that sense of "I" within you. You may close your eyes from time to time as you please. Feel your body, move your shoulders and stand up straight and feel good about your body. Check out your arms, shake your legs and move around. Genuinely focus on yourself: only think about your existence and the sense of self. What does that 'I' actually mean to you? Just focus on yourself, explore your body and keep asking who that self is and what his/her roles and responsibilities are. Basically – ask yourself;

1. What do 'I' actually do?
2. What are my duties, to whom and why?
3. Ask what am I doing and how am I doing it?
4. How well do I know that sense of 'I' separate from my body and how close am I to knowing it?

The idea of questioning the boundaries of self may appear to some as a strange act to follow. Truthfully, how often do we ever consciously sit down and question these fundamental topics that directly relate to our absolute essence and the reasons for us being here and now. How often do we question such things and to what depth do we go to find the truth?

We generally tend to deal reactively with what life throws at us and we hardly ever find time to seriously question the **'Big WHY'**. We often continue to do just what we do day-in-day out mainly based on what we are familiar with and what we believe is possible. But strangely, we somehow always surprise ourselves when our experiences, the ones that are born out of our own imagination and the ones we are going through, appear and feel unpleasant and out of place to us. We may feel trapped in a reality which unconsciously we keep on creating. Similar events, relationships and experiences keep on repeating themselves at which point we begin to recognise a repeatable pattern.

To get away from this endless loop, we need to 'be genuinely interested in improving ourselves, ask the questions that really matter, eagerly crave to learn and always try to change ourselves for better'. Our only way out of a given problem is firstly by not doing what we have been doing to date. We need to think differently and act differently in order to get out of the pattern of where we are; otherwise we keep on repeating the same experiment and expecting different results (Albert Einstein).

If you logically think about it, the concept of intelligence is very much about the required human capability for assessing his/her position within the context of one's surrounding environment and how to successfully react to the unfolding events so the self and the extension of self (such as family, community, etc.) are sustainably benefited. The final outcome from such a process allows people to benefit, firstly by surviving well in a given environment and secondly, fairly contributing to their immediate family, community and the larger environment.

Basically, we are here (the 'I' in the machine) to contribute to our world and beyond and in order to do that, we need an able and a functioning body to effectively achieve this for us. Therefore, common sense tells us that we need to look after the body which directly enables our contributions and interactions with life. So to be fair to the body/ your only tool and machine in this world, please feed it well, exercise it with loving care and give it ample rest so the next day, it can get up, get to work and do what you really want it to do – your interactions and contributions to the world. So the question for us is, how do we use our bodies/ our machines in achieving various outcomes in our lives and what are we meant to achieve that really matter to us in life, both directly and indirectly through our contribution to the larger community.

> The purpose of life is to contribute in some way to making things better.
> **—Robert F. Kennedy**

> The sole meaning of life is to serve humanity.
> **—Leo Tolstoy**

The Scope and Focus of 'I'

If we assume that the real 'I' in us is like a driver who cannot live outside its machine/ body and only experiences life through the machine's senses and capabilities. Then we need to ask the question – if this 'I' has very little idea of how this machine is built and operates, then what does this 'I' actually control and what functions are beyond its control?

What does this 'I' directly control?

I am sure you would agree with me that our commands are obeyed by various parts in our bodies'. The list is made up of our sensory parts (ears, eyes, mouth, sense of taste and touch), motor parts (arms, legs, voice, mouth, etc.). Please note most of these capabilities can be used for both sensing and motor functions (for example, mouth can be opened to receive food or spit or eyes can be used to sense what is out there and also they can blink to communicate with the outside world).

What does this 'I' not directly control?

The operations of internal organs (For example, the digestive system).Even though we are responsible for them as we can help or damage them at will, they are truly beyond our (the 'I's') intelligence and direct control. Even though we are responsible for them, we don't have enough knowledge of their amazing complexities. For this reason we can't directly control them. For example, we can't move our kidneys or tell our liver how to process things.

How should the 'I' see its roles?

Before we can use our machine appropriately and effectively, we need to first know what the actual purpose and the needs of the 'I' are, secondly what satisfies these needs, thirdly where this 'I' is situated (what are the rules that governs it) and fourthly, how should this 'I' act (what works & deliver value).

What is the purpose of 'I' in this world?

It is really fascinating to note that the entire social world is structured around how best we should serve the body. Everything we watch on official media is very much based on how we should look, what to wear, what life style we should have and in general how to create creature comforts around ourselves. Most social products are created to pamper the body through various luxuries we are told we need to purchase. Starting from birth to old age and even in retirement we are sold products to assist with our death, burial or after life care.

There is hardly ever an organised social opportunity to have open debates, public encouragement to explore and provide official education about our <u>individual purpose</u> in life (what our body is here to achieve and contribute to life). We have been so deeply conditioned by social engineers to stay in this sleep like state of social norms that we hardly think about why we actually exist at all.

In examining the purpose of 'I', we also need to question the overall purpose of life. Does life have a purpose to fulfil and if so for whom and why?

> The two most important days in your life are the day you are born and the day you find out why.
>
> **—Mark Twain**

Micro's Ignorance of Macro's Context & Purpose
From an individual 'I' perspective (macro view of the body) looking at his/ her body, the only purpose cells in the body have is just to serve the body by cooperating and systemically working with other cells in order to make the overall body function effectively. However, this purpose (cell is there to serve the 'I') is not necessarily shared or consciously understood by

individual cells in the body. For example, if you (the macro body) could tell a single cell in your body that the reason it (the cell) exists is to work with other cells and collaborate so the overall body (you) can survive and function in a healthy, prosperous and efficient way. Since the cell cannot consciously be aware of such macro perspectives imposed upon it, if the cells could talk back to you, it would probably say that its purpose (in its own language) is just to stay alive in a nice style and enjoy itself anyway possible. It may not even be aware that it belongs to a larger body (the 'I' body). It just helps itself with whatever it knows at its local level.

This is similar to the purpose of a person from the larger community and the wider world perspective. If you say to people that the real purpose for their existence is only to serve the community they belong to and they need to do this in order for the overall community and ultimately the world/ universe to continue to be successful, healthy and functional. As you can imagine, people may violently object to such notions and would not accept the imposed higher big brother expectations upon them. They may see the purpose for their existence as whatever they individually wish to decide and the kind of things they believe that can make them happy, meeting their personal needs and basically doing whatever they want in life. They would not like to see themselves as a cog in a machine with a predefined intended destiny/ purpose for serving a bigger body or system.

We could view a typical cell in the body to operate in an opportunistic manner rather than being driven by a higher intention or being devoted to a larger body/system which is there to control it. The cells cooperation/ contribution are in exchange for benefits they receive from their environments. From our macro 'I' perspective, If our cells refuse to contribute to the body, they become a burden to the overall health and wellbeing of the big body and similar to unwelcomed viruses, they just take from the body mercilessly whatever they can and provide nothing back in return. This of course weakens or causes serious damage to the body's state of health and capability.

Although a cell's conscious awareness may not understand or appreciate the bigger body that it belongs to, it would certainly be conscious of its own smaller components (smaller sub cells) which make up its total body (the cell). These smaller components of a given cell would also follow the same pattern and would not consciously realise they belong to the cell. Therefore this holographic pattern (macro <u>conscious awareness</u> of the micro level and the micro <u>unconscious awareness</u> of the macro level) will endlessly repeat itself at every level of existence.

> Everyone has been made for some particular work, and the desire for that work has been put in every heart.
>
> **—Rumi**

Macro Conscious Ignorance of the Micro's Intelligence

For example, if you asked a person how do you control and manage your internal organs? In all honesty, the only answer he or she could give is that I really don't know how my organs work, their intelligence and how they do what they do in my body is beyond my comprehension. The person will just say that I am allowed to use my body in exchange for the food and rest I provide to it through my social intelligence and engagement with the world. So in search of real answers, we go to the organs, for example, we go to the liver and we ask the consciously aware part of the liver (the "I" of the liver) how it actually manages such great laboratory and intelligence within its confinement. The conscious 'I' liver probably responds that – I really don't know how my parts within me work. As the conscious 'I' of the liver, I am just responsible for the liver, but I really don't know how it works internally within me. It would suggest to us that we need to go and talk to its components and they would have the answers for how they intelligently do their work and manage the functions of the liver. As you can imagine, the deeper you go, the more you realise that no conscious level in the entire body has any real understanding of how things within it actually work, as if the entire body works at the smallest granular level simply by magic.

Therefore what should matter most to the concept of 'I' is not about mastering its understanding of how it's biological or mechanical 'body suit' (the body) works. It is about how effectively the 'I' should use the body that is given to it to achieve the true purpose of 'I' for being on this planet. The 'I' should let the body/ machine just be as the body knows best how to intelligently manage and heal itself and all the 'I' has to do is just consciously look after the body well (provide food, comfort, exercise and rest). The 'I' should focus and use its conscious intelligence to effectively achieve what the 'I' is meant to do within its systemic and social context.

Quality of Life within the Systemic & Changing World

As the Eurythmics song says 'everybody is looking for something'. What is it we are looking for in life? The best way to describe the quality of life is 'by not focusing on the objects we desire or want to see and have in our lives, but focus on the <u>experiences</u> that we wish to have with those objects. Basically what experiences will make us happy. Happiness is not just to be in possession of objects and things. It is about our <u>interaction and experiences</u> with them.

What is important to us?

If we ask people what is important to them in life, as you can imagine, everybody will express their views differently. Things such as:

- I live for my kids and I want the best for them, their happiness wellbeing, etc.;
- Personal wealth, power and knowledge;

- Happy love life and rich relationship;
- Being able to achieve whatever, etc.

From the social and psychological definition (people like Milton Rockeach), what we individually regard as important to us are our values. Some of these values are like a destination for us (they are called 'Terminal Values') such as 'Sense of accomplishment', 'a comfortable life', 'an exciting life', 'Family security' and so on. Other types of Values that we hold dear to our hearts relate to how we should behave while we are trying to get to our destinations (they are called Instrumental Values) such as 'Honesty', 'Honour', 'Kindness' or 'Courage', etc.

Peace of mind

What we must realise is that behind every desire and action we have, there is an underlying motive and a higher intention. So basically the reason that I want this or that, it is because, in that experience of engaging with the object of desire, it will make me feel wonderful, alive, happy, complete and satisfied and unless I have that (the experience of WOW), I am not going to rest, would feel empty, anxious and mentally nagged until I have that WOW experience. Think it as a common form of addiction which we all strive for – the WOW experience.

Basically Instrumental Values are means
to an end. The end is the quality of life
(Terminal Values) that we seek.

Example: Whatever we do in terms of achieving things in life is for that WOW, for example, you are mowing the lawn and tiding up the garden in an effort to 'make a good impression on your friends visiting you' is a value you regard as important. You do all the hard work so when friends are standing on your lawn and having a glass of wine, you can look around and say **YES** (I feel great because it looks great & <u>I can relax now</u> and enjoy myself – WOW). So that feeling of happiness and satisfaction is what we want in everything we do – WOW.

So the highest quality for our existence, the thing we deeply seek is that state of serenity and sense of satisfaction. It is that peace of mind. So the ultimate quality of life for us is to feel that state of happiness, balance and harmony rather than feel anxious, restless and worried. So what we achieve (those values) are only a means to an end and the end is that sense of joy and empowerment.

We all naturally gravitate towards a sense of joy and completeness. These desires are natural to us and run in our blood. We are literally **pleasure seeking creatures**.

Encountering the absence of Peace of mind

It would also be fair to say that in spite of our hard work and diligence, we are not always guaranteed to experience that sense of joy and peace (WOW).

For example, you can have many things in life, but feel deprived of experiencing that deep state of satisfaction. That is why we keep looking for more things, new things in life in the hope that state of inner satisfaction can somehow be bridged. You don't have to go far, if you look at the western world, you will see lots of wealth and material goods, but unfortunately you don't necessary see many smiling faces or truly satisfied people. I am sure we can all relate to that in spite of our achievements and the presence of physical objects all around us, many of us still feel that sense of emptiness, void, restlessness as if things are not quite the way we expect them to be. We often feel that we are not getting a deep sense of happiness or satisfaction.

Of course, I am not saying there is anything wrong with material things in life as they have their own relevant place and should not be ignored. What I am saying is that if the quality of my life is the key factor and driver in my life, then I must consciously place a great emphasis and focus on whatever capabilities I can muster up that can ultimately enhance and deliver my peace of mind. In other word, I should not mindlessly pursue objects in the hope of experiencing happiness.

World of Change
What does Quality of Life (sense of aliveness) mean within the context of our day-to-day systemic and changing world? If we look at our lives, we notice that almost everything around us is in a state of change and that is a given. Life constantly dishes out all sorts of both desirable and undesirable situations for us to

deal with. Therefore we can't escape from this state of existence. This is how it is. From the systematic nature of our world, we are totally integrated with everything and everyone around us.

> Life is a series of natural and spontaneous changes. Do not resist. Let them move forward in whatever way they like.
>
> **—Lao Tzu**

Micro & Macrocosms

As a child I was mesmerised by the concept of real magic and I learnt at an early age that one of the pivotal laws that supports the fundamental concept of magic is the perspective of Macrocosm and Microcosm which means what is below is what is above and what is above is what is within. Of course, in those days, this view was seen by the main stream as mumbo jumbo and now, of course it is regarded as part of main stream science. The Systems Sciences such as systems theory, Cybernetics, Holographic and the chaos theory (fractal concept), they all fully subscribe to the notion of Macrocosm and Microcosm. As if the scientific community is showing great signs of catching up with ancient wisdom. To understand this, we need to realise that we individually (as an organism) are like systems, we have inputs/ outputs: that means we receive from our world and we interact with our world through our activities, there are many systems within me such as my heart, liver, lungs, etc. I am also part of a larger system such as my community, earth, the solar system, the Milky Way and the universe. So we belong to many micro and macro structures and systems. We can infinitely go down to the world of atoms within us and look at it as a system and we could also go above to other larger celestial and extra celestial systems: everything follows the same concept of micro and macro holographic structures.

Basically, as long as we are alive, we need to interact with the changing life around us, because in this systemic universe, we are woven and integrated within the fabric of life. For this reason, we cannot avoid the changes that are coming our way. We need to intelligently assimilate the incoming changes one way or another.

Of course, we may choose to reduce or increase our interactions with our world (Ashby's law of Requisite Variety), but still we have to interact with life one way or another and we cannot avoid the concept of a changing world as long as we live.

Can we have Peace of mind?
The question is that since we are here, can we be part of this amazing life, can we immerse ourselves totally into life and have a rich and healthy interaction with it and at the same time maintain our peace of mind, experience that sense of togetherness, feel fulfilled, coherent in our thoughts and our actions. Is it possible for me to be happier, more alive and more connected with life? I believe it is absolutely possible

and the potential for individuals reaching that state of happiness and togetherness is totally dependent on how much they <u>allow their individual expansion for learning to progress</u>.

The more we open up to new possibilities, consciously increase our self-awakening process and live to know, we create more opportunities for ourselves to wisely reflect and subsequently create more potential for manifesting and experiencing total human liberation and happier social existence.

If we constantly exclude the inflow of new possibilities into our lives, we will directly inhibit our potential for attaining and preserving our quality of life. That is the reason why so many of us continue to endorse and accept our everyday frustration, misery, and unhappiness, day in day out, because, we don't know any better or 'that is all we know'.

Since we are all pleasure seeking creatures and want to be happy, at peace and satisfied, no one deliberately or consciously sets out to choose suffering as the best possible option. Therefore, if I am continuing to put up with my ongoing anger, frustration and unhappiness, that must mean that such a miserable daily selection must be the only valid option for me and that out of all possible options available, I can only choose the ones I know or am accustomed to. Therefore in the absence of new options and possibilities, we keep gravitating to the same negative feelings and sufferings and they become our normal state of being and of course our sufferings will continue to our next day.

Remember, if we keep doing the same thing day in day out, we shall experience exactly the same result day in day out. The only way we can change our situation is to open up and learn new possibilities.

If we are not receiving, we are denying the fact that we are part of this systemic world. We need to expand and open up to possibilities. Remember –the potential for individuals reaching that state of happiness and togetherness is totally dependent on how much they allow their individual expansion for learning to progress.

If I knew more, would I change my life for better, would I consider seeing reality beyond just my personal context, would I act differently to improve my life? The answer is **YES**.

> Progress is impossible without change,
> and those who cannot change their minds
> cannot change anything.
>
> **—George Bernard Shaw**

Quality of intelligence

What do we mean by human intelligence?

Intelligence is human ability that allows us to read our environment, analyse, adjust/adapt and react to our world purely based on what matters to us and is deeply valued. For example, our survival, assets, goals, aspirations, convictions, sustainable prosperity, etc.

I am not saying that we need a special gift before we can act intelligently such as knowing advanced mathematics or the ability to think like great men of science. It is much simpler than that: it is about common sense.

We all act intelligently every second. We have intelligent components and ability built into our bodies. We all have intelligent machines within us that work diligently all the time. We are all doing it all the time. Even animals are intelligent machines. If we are reacting to our environment, we are using our intelligent capabilities.

The components of our intelligence are our senses for reading what is within and what is around us, our rational analytical capabilities and our physical actions.

Why do we need to pay attentions to our intelligence?

We have established that we are intelligent, so what is a big deal that we need to pay attention to it? We know that the quality of our lives is directly based on our intelligence. For this reason, we all need to pay attention to the quality of our intelligence as it dictates the quality of our lives.

For example; you are at your local pub celebrating your birthday with two close friends – John and Mary. As you are having a great time, all of a sudden, you are provoked and insulted by an unreasonable drunk in the pub. Based on your quality of intelligence, you may respond to the situation by punching the person and knock him over. And by accident, he could bang his head, get seriously hurt or at worse, die. So the consequence of exercising your intelligence could be very costly on your psyche and your social life. On the other hand, John in the same situation could just turn back from the situation, walk away and go home. He might be internally very upset and have internal fights and potentially create an unresolved issue inside himself and have a restless night. But his intelligence prevented him having more serious social consequences. Mary, on the other hand, uses her intelligence very differently and instead of fighting, she simply talks to the drunk and manages to calm him down, gets an apology and a free drink. Her intelligence allowed her to have the peace of mind, a free drink and potentially a friend out of her actions.

The question is, can we tune this intelligent machine of ours to work more optimally and create a better world for us individually and collectively? The answer is absolutely YES and you shall see why as we progress.

What fuels and controls our intelligence?

So if we are going to increase the quality of our intelligence what do we do? First we need to understand what impacts the effective use of our intelligence either positively or negatively?

One thing we can say is that the quality of our intelligence is not dependent on the quality of our abilities. More or less, we have similar computer hardware; however the software that runs within each computer is different. Most of us are fortunate to possess sensory capabilities (For example, eyes, ears, touch, etc.) These senses allow us to get input from our world. Similarly, we have motor capabilities such as arms, legs and voice to interact with the world that surrounds us. Even if we don't have every single limb or functioning sensory capabilities, we generally compensate either through other senses or artificial means. That should not change the quality of our intelligence. A good example of this is the brilliant astrophysicist – Steven Hawkins who has severe motor deficiencies, yet possesses a highly elevated level and quality of intelligence. Therefore we should remove our emphasis on our anatomy and explore what actually influences and drives our intelligence.

The quality of our intelligence is totally dependent on the quality of beliefs we each internally hold about the world around us. For example, in the above example of a drunk in the pub, your quality of intelligence led you to go to jail. All because you held the belief that <u>no one should bully you and get away with it</u>. Mary on the other hand had a belief that <u>people in general are innocent</u> and the reason for them misbehaving is due to their past conditioning and life circumstances. So she wasn't setting out to punish anyone, she wanted to engage and use her communication skills to resolve the situation.

Quality of Beliefs

What is a belief?

The internal programs/ rules that govern our intelligence in the way it allows us to sense, rationalise and act. We see the world based on what we want to see, how we believe it impacts us and how we believe we should act and engage with the world.

It is very important to know ourselves, our make-up and how our beliefs govern us. Once we have a better sense of understanding our internal drivers, then we begin to understand others better and find it easier to forgive them and deal with them more effectively. In such an environment of awareness, we can see new horizons and feel empowered to create new options that we did not have before. For example, we can:

- Understand the reasons behind our self-inflicted stresses & sufferings.
- Learn how to apply our powers of imagination in order to cure our day-to-day problems including our physical health.

By using our current beliefs and needs, we draw conclusions from what we encounter and substantiate reasons to create a new set of beliefs. The thoughts and conclusions that result from our beliefs and views on life's events always and without exception generate emotions and our brains translate such emotions into a matching neuropeptide protein chain that will travel and reach every cell within our body and directly impact our whole body positively or negatively. For example, anger manifests in every cell in our body. This is why we need to have quality beliefs about ourselves and life in order to generate empowering and energising chemicals that can serve our cells positively and enhance our wellbeing. In the following chapters we shall discuss in detail how our beliefs influence us on a daily basis.

12.

Understanding the power of our beliefs in shaping our world paradigm

To know our individual positions in this amazing life, first we truly need to know our own mind and our inner essence. We must understand and appreciate the mind's incredible hidden powers and energies which constantly operate within us, attracting or repulsing people, objects and events into our daily lives.

Why can't we consciously be happy and who is really in charge of our happiness?

We hardly ever look at the possibility that we can deliberately exercise our personal powers for choosing happiness in whatever scenarios we may encounter in life. I guess we are often too busy with life and we actually lose sight and forget what actually matters to us most. Can we consciously choose to be happy on a daily basis instead of feeling sad about our life experiences and encounters?

If we have the choice to be happy, then we need to seriously question why the majority of us choose misery and unhappiness on a daily basis. Surely our personal happiness is one of the most important reasons for our existence and as a matter of fact the pursuit of happiness is what actually drives us in life, isn't it? If we are genuinely seeking happiness, then we should legitimately question and understand why we often feel paralysed to exercise our rights and consciously choose happiness in life.

As we all know, there are many stressed and unhappy people all around us and we don't have to look hard as they are everywhere. You can see grim faces at work, in social encounters, family gatherings and often at home with our loved ones. There is no doubt that every single person in this world ultimately wishes for happiness. The question is why they can't consciously choose happiness and why they become addicted to their misery, sorrow and grief instead?

Is there a hidden part within us that goes against the natural grain of our being, desires, wishes and somehow prevents us from being happy? Why on earth such a part possesses more power than our conscious self and why does it deliberately derail us from experiencing happiness in life?

To explore such a strange human anomaly, I am going to propose three interesting questions and investigate how we actually make choices in our heads. In this examination, I shall reveal to you some surprising discrepancies that exist between the way we consciously desire things in life and the way we often unconsciously go about not achieving them. That is to say, we end up behaving in such a conflicting way that ensures we never achieve those desires that we set out to obtain. In other words our choices somehow do not necessarily support what we desire and set out to accomplish in life. Such inconsistencies truly deserve further explanation, especially for those of us who are adamant and subscribe to the notion of free will. OK let's explore what I mean here.

Point-1: Do you believe that people in general are pleasure seeking creatures and they consciously dislike being in pain or experience negative feelings such as sadness or anger? I am sure you all agree this to be true for the majority of us. No one consciously likes pain. One could argue that even the masochist, at the end, is driven by the sense of pleasure they obtain through their particular actions and they just don't want pain for the sake of experiencing pain.

Point- 2: Do you also agree that the majority of people truly believe they have free will and they can choose whatever they wish on their own terms? This implies that no factors can interfere with their conscious decisions and they can remain totally objective in how they make their choices. Society always reminds us that we have free will. That plays an important role in our judicial system. You basically pay for your choices.

Point-3: Do you also agree that out of every experience or scenario in life, we can either have a negative or positive reaction to the event? There are two possibilities we can have in every scenario, either to be Ok with it and not let your overall quest for happiness in life become quashed by the event or, conversely, feel sad and miserable.

Disregarding the severity of the event we encounter, we can either, laugh about it, view it calmly, objectively, consider it philosophically and feel at peace with it or we could feel devastated, take it badly and become miserable or sad about it.

If you agree with the points I have just described, then how would you really explain why the majority of people, given they have free will and they seek happiness, actually end up choosing misery and suffering day in day out in preference to choosing happiness or being at peace? Disregarding the individual's level of wealth, health or station in life, how many people do you know who are constantly struggling with their daily life and experiencing negative emotions as a normal state of being?

The answer to such mental discrepancy lies in the power of our subconscious mind over our conscious objectivity and the way our subconscious makes decisions without us consciously being there or involved in any aspect of it. We genuinely think that we are objective and in charge and have free will, but this is far from the truth of how we operate internally. There is a great misconception about our <u>Conscious Objectivity</u> in life that is hardly ever discussed in open social forums.

The majority of us innocently believe that we objectively and consciously control and make decisions about our daily life events. This general misapprehension is primarily due to the fact that most people have no real comprehension of how life concepts get established and processed in their heads. Since we all like to be the master of our own destinies, it is somewhat convenient for us to assume that we are fully in charge of our lives.

The truth is that very few people have any deep awareness of their true make up, their sense of self, what drives them, where and how their beliefs come to be and how their subconscious **"likes and dislikes"** influence their perceptions, thoughts and actions both positively and negatively. The subconscious mind – that is where our individual beliefs reside is a place where our conscious mind is not permitted to probe freely. Our conscious mind is not allowed to regulate or have any control over the way our emotions are made in our subconscious factory.

Our emotions are the subconscious conclusions to life events or encounters and these emotions directly guide how we consciously perceive things, how we make decisions and how we act in life. Such mental configuration explains why in spite our genuine desire for happiness most of us generally end up choosing misery or sadness.

In order to get somewhere closer to the notion of conscious or free choices, first we need to consciously become awakened, witness and override the interplay of our subconscious biases. In the next section I explain further how we can objectively rewire ourselves, to grow intelligently and respond to our constantly changing world for better.

Do we become cerebrally limited by the intensity of our beliefs?

Is it possible for us to become intellectually and cerebrally cheated by the intensity of the beliefs we hold in our heads? Can we become blinded by our over powering beliefs and subsequently pay for them dearly in life?

How many people do you actually know who consciously challenge their core foundations of thinking and behaviour on a continuous basis? Most of us never go there as we often innocently buy into to the idea that we are one and the same with our thoughts.

We are generally convinced that if it is in our heads, then it must officially exist and is legitimate. We often proudly claim 'this is what or who I am' which generally highlights our lack of curiosity for knowing what actually makes us internally tick in life and it may also be a way of saying to ourselves and others that 'we are not prepared to question or change ourselves if we can help it'.

This explains why many people would rather live with their daily suffering while unconsciously holding tight to their current ways of being, the ones that are potentially responsible for their suffering in the first place. Many of us hardly question our social conditioning or give ourselves a real chance to organically evolve and rationally refine our ways of being for the better.

We cannot escape from the fact that whatever we individually believe or strongly embrace in our heads will fundamentally drive our behaviour in life. Through such an internal lens, we:

Firstly – observe the world around us, recognise potential values or threats;

Secondly – pass judgement on people, situations and the environment; and

Thirdly – make decisions and react to our emerging circumstances in order to maximise our chance of survival and improve on our long term prosperity in life.

Whether we like it or not, for all our daily interactions in life, we are truly at the mercy of such internal subconscious conditioning.

For this reason we need to pay conscious attention to what we actually hold in our heads and often innocently perceive as our personal reality and the reality of what is around us. Now let's look at how our beliefs are established and become entrenched in our psyche.

As we go through life, we subjectively learn from our daily encounters and such information is generally based on our existing beliefs at the time of the event, combined with what we personally feel about the impact of the experiences that we go through. Ultimately our individual learning and conclusions from encounters in life shape the overall mental picture of how we should see and interact with the world around us.

Such a personal mental picture unconsciously establishes our foundations for general cognition and our internal hardwiring in how we may evaluate future encounters and feel compelled to react to them. The new information from our experiences will eventually become our emergent beliefs and subsequently reshape our current mental picture.

It is important to note that our newly acquired beliefs are almost always derived from and reinforced by our prior beliefs as if we subconsciously feel compelled or driven to build upon the foundations of what we currently know, rather than start new foundations in contrast to our current beliefs. As human beings we have a general tendency not to repeat the same learning experiment too many times. So, as best as we can, we try to capitalise on our earlier learning investments rather than start afresh and unbiasedly force ourselves to remain totally open minded with each situation.

This means that as we get older, we unconsciously become more and more entrenched and resistant to new concepts that may potentially force us to up root our dearly guarded foundations and ultimately push us to challenge our current ways and beliefs. As an easy option, we would rather stick to what we know as our ongoing perceived reality. This also explains why the majority of people increase their resistance to change as they progressively get older.

If we are constantly driven by our beliefs, then how can we really gauge the validity of what we hold in our heads? How do we actually know if such internal views represent the truth about our particular life dynamics and environment or whether these views can intelligently enable our cognitive evaluations and help us apply fit for purpose solutions to our life situations? Since our beliefs are heavily influenced by the biases of our subconscious and often in a partial or total absence of our conscious presence, therefore, our inner perception about the soundness of our personal beliefs is highly questionable.

Our minds can easily be tricked and become subtly controlled by intentional suggestions either from unconscious influences or the influence of others around us. It is interesting to note that every individual regards their personal beliefs to be more valid and potentially closer to the absolute truth than other beliefs that may be in contrast to their view points. So for the sake of thinking and acting intelligently, we should never consider any of our beliefs as the ultimate truth, but view them merely as a potential possibility for the truth.

Which beliefs should we question?
Generally speaking, all beliefs may be regarded as valid in their own particular context as each one is a given interpretation of the absolute reality that can never be accurately or objectively measured. The concept of reality is only a subjective phenomenon.

Therefore there is no such thing as an absolute or reliable general truth.

However, we could say that if things in life are not working well for an individual, then the root causes of such a perceived reality can directly be attributed to certain beliefs that are not serving that individual well. In other words, if we are struggling to sustainably meet our needs, if we feel compromised to interact intelligently and respond to our changing environment, then we need to consciously narrow down those beliefs that are causally responsible for such behavioural shortfalls. We then need to genuinely examine them and appropriately change them to create a new reality for ourselves.

Disregarding the level of conviction we may hold for our existing beliefs or what we may think about their appropriateness in our lives, it is always in our best interest to truthfully question their legitimacy and validity, especially if they appear to have negative or limiting consequences on our opportunities in life. We need to keep an open mind on all potential outlooks and concepts that may capture our attention in this world and see them all as possible candidate beliefs for our intelligent evaluation and selection.

As much as possible we must resist the emotional urge for a hasty dismissal of the contrasting views we encounter. We should not conveniently hang on to what we currently know or feel attached to as the ultimate truth as this will limit our options. The unbiased assessment of our reality will help us to create an intelligent basis for all our daily activities and endeavours.

It is always liberating to prove to ourselves that we are in pursuit of a moving and ever changing truth rather than feeling ignorantly stuck in a fixed fantasy or a socially borrowed position. We need to openly investigate our beliefs in order to ensure we are intelligently informed and behaving responsibly for our own personal sake, the sake of our families and the larger community.

Look at the world of chaos around us and it is all because people are unconsciously driven to fight tooth and nail for their borrowed perspectives: For things such as, my social, political or religious views are better or bigger than yours. We literally kill one another ignorantly for our never questioning beliefs. How sad and ignorant is that. We need to question our beliefs rationally and objectively rather than emotionally justifying their unconscious hold on us or worst, legitimise their unconditional existence.

We must refuse to take the least resistant path in our investigations. As best we can, we need to investigate the circumstances in which our beliefs were established and formed as our internal binding reality. We must question if they were based on mature assessment of the situation at the time and if they were sensibly based on a plausible set of facts.

Consequences of blindly accepting our beliefs

For example, you may establish a biased belief when you are 2 years old and such a belief can innocently drive you to perceive and act ignorantly for your entire life and consequently cause you an untold amount of avoidable suffering. If such a biased belief is intelligently identified early in a piece, questioned and addressed promptly, you may potentially prevent yourself from many years of unnecessary pain and missed opportunities.

It is always wise to question our level of maturity and the information that we consider at the time we drew our life influencing conclusions and established our life lasting beliefs. Whatever mental configuration we may choose to embrace and come to accept as our reality will ultimately influence and drive us day-in-day-out for the rest of our lives.

For example, if I have a fear of certain social situations, I owe it to myself to liberate myself by learning more about the reason for my limiting attitude. I should be curious to know the validity of the underlying beliefs that support such negative behaviour. I need to question the time when I formed such debilitating views and what level of wisdom or maturity I applied in support of such views in the first place. I should ask myself how old I was, what did I actually know about life at that time and how broad was my vision on my subjective reality?

If I have adopted certain beliefs in the way I judge certain group of people, or the way I easily become annoyed by their behaviour or certain situations, it is in my best interest to discover if such views were intelligently based. I need to pause and question if I am just blindly acting out on my limited reality without fully understanding the actual root causes for my negative behaviour and the causal consequences of my action on my personal life and other lives that I directly impact.

How can we end our daily struggles for being negative?

Well, changing beliefs in the way we interact in life mean that our life experiences will also change accordingly. Then if we are currently struggling with life in our current mind set, our struggles will end if we use a different mind-set. The only way our daily struggles may be addressed is certainly not by us continuing with what we have always been doing. The problems can only be remedied by us doing something different and in order to do that, first we need to change the beliefs that drive our current behaviour.

Therefore the less we allow ourselves to consider other potential perspectives and candidate beliefs; things within the overall mix of the available potential, the less we evolve as individuals, community or nation. It is bad enough to be totally sold and view our existing faiths or beliefs as the ultimate definition of our reality, it is far worse to fight bitterly over them and alienate others around ourselves. Disregarding how right we may think our current beliefs are, by hanging on only to one set of possibilities, we naturally limit our overall potential in life simply by excluding other sets of possibilities, narrowing our expansion for learning and limit the evolution of our natural development.

Your true prosperity lies in the mastery of your subconscious mind

Misconception about our Conscious Objectivity

What we need to realise is that when we confront a life event, our subconscious emotional reaction to the event, automatically results in the release of its matching chemicals (For example, sadness, anger, etc.) into every cell in our bodies. This activity takes place without our conscious involvement as if consciously we have no say in that. Once we consciously become aware of the feeling in our bodies it will be almost too late for us in such a situation to remain objective whilst the corresponding chemical emotions are directly influencing and biasing our perspectives.

The person undergoing such experiences (most people and most of the time) will feel an unfolding force of emotional change in his/ her entire being. One can almost instantly taste the emotion and feel the alterations in their energy field. Once these powerful chemicals are experienced in the body, the conscious mind will find it extremely difficult to reason objectively and to examine the unfolding life events from the position of greater and unbiased understanding. There is no way that the conscious mind can rationally disengage itself from "how it deeply feels" – which is the emotional substance presented by the subconscious (emotions at the cellular level in the body).

Shortfalls of Logically Structured therapies

The problem begins when the conscious mind tries to look for answers within the context of its emotional biases. Wherever it looks for answers, it only sees the world from emotionally painted views. In the majority of cases, our claim for conscious derivations of meanings in a given situation is merely another way of legitimising and endorsing our earlier emotional conclusions and nothing else. We do it under the disguise that we are rationally engaged, thinking straight and being objective.

This is why many practitioners, with the best of intentions, struggle to bring about desired changes in their patients/ clients when they resort to logical reasoning as their only means for healing the subconscious wounds. The application of cognitive therapies for an emotionally charged person is a wasteful pursuit. No matter how many times we try to help people through logical discussions, their emotionally influenced body would not have a bar of anything outside their emotional context, especially when they are already overpowered by such emotional chemicals.

How to look for Solutions

Therefore in order to have a clear head to look for the holistic truth in our encounters in life and derive a real solution that can enable, empower and prosper us individually and collectively; we must somehow prevent the high intensity emotional feeling from being released within our mind in the first place.

This suggests that in order to be truly liberated from the biases of the subconscious and live a free, conscious and happy life, we must heal our subconscious from its short sightedness and its emotional chemical influences. We must make it our business to turn those negative, unproductive beliefs about who we are and how we should live and act in this world to a wiser set of beliefs that are aligned with our state of happiness and wellbeing. We need to consciously bring about change to our current beliefs that are no longer serving us and create a holistic understanding of the bigger context, a healthy and balanced approach to life.

Through the processes of conscious self-healing intentions and actions, we begin to clean from our minds the unnecessary disempowering beliefs and begin to embrace openness to life; our subconscious suddenly stops generating negative emotions because it does not derive untrue/ manufactured conclusions. Subsequently we will find ourselves more energised, in charge and happy.

However, it is important to note that the subconscious is always ready to exert itself as the ruler and change the progress of our liberation and for this, the journey of Conscious mind empowerment over the Subconscious should be an on ongoing activity similar to daily remembrance and meditation.

Conscious living tips

The following points can help the reader to develop ways of empowering his/ her conscious thoughts and maintain control over their subconscious mind moods.

1. **Stay conscious most of the time** – This means listen to the internal voice as if there is another person present in your head making conversation with you (your Subconscious). You will know if you are in your conscious zone, when you are unbiased, liberal in attitude and curious for the sake of knowing the truth disregarding of its consequences or applications. In this zone you can experience and view **human Feelings only** as a **momentary phenomenon** and you are consciously willing to allow the generated feelings to set aside in order for you to grasp real objectivity from your deeper perception.

   We all have the capability to fall in and out of conscious awareness. However, some of us, through lack of understanding and exposure, have little to no desire to experience this. Others with prior exposure and understanding of conscious ways frequently enjoy the benefits of viewing the world from this position of clarity and openness.

   It is a sad fact that most of us are hardly conscious at all, even though we genuinely think we are. Of course, we all have consciousness, but it is usually an un-questioning and obedient servant to the Subconscious. Very seldom does our conscious mind actually take the initiative to stand up and declare its independence and exercise its kingly presence. Most of the time, whatever comes to the consciousness from the subconscious is treated as fact and in a robotic fashion, the conscious immediately follows through to either justify its emotional conditioning or actually carrying through what it has been instructed to do. For those who wish to experience their conscious awareness, they should try various popular techniques for quieting their minds, such as meditation or self-hypnosis.

2. **Resist completing the picture of what you are Feeling** – You can objectively watch the subconscious emotions rising within you and if you wish, you can also consciously refuse to embrace them as they could have side effects and blind your objectivity. You should seek to know the absolute truth and search for it with everything you have. Do not try to justify and prove what appears as **'gut feelings'** or any other feelings produced in your head. It is often hard to distinguish between the emotions produced by the subconscious with its corresponding biases and other mysterious divine sources of truth (intuition). For this reason, look at everything objectively as imposters and disguisers are often hard to unveil.

   For example: You have just met your new boss and he begins to explain his expectations of you in this new role. Without knowing why, you may immediately feel a sense of insecurity/ fear rising

within you. Even though the presented direc-
tives, at least on the surface, may be reasonable
and are within the domain of your capability.
Based on your subconscious fears, you may exaggerate and complete the picture in your head as
hard challenges and ones that could stretch you
beyond your comfort zones. If you could isolate
the initial fears and look at what you have been
asked to perform in an emotionless and objective
way, you may complete this picture very differently with a sense of ease and self-empowerment.
The issue for negative emotions rising from the
'subconscious' could be due to the fact that your
new boss's expression or tone of voice may have
been referenced against your subconscious view of
your father that you could never please and were
constantly scared of. Your new boss may have no
real correlations to your dad, but you feel a sense
of fear in his presence. This example highlights
how much misunderstanding and confusion can
spring up in what we perceive as reality and what
the actual reality is in the domain of our minds
(conscious & subconscious). Such commonly
occurring human misunderstanding decreases
our overall coherence, can increase our daily stress
levels, takes away our real objectivity for intelligent
decision making and can weaken the effectiveness
of our actions.

3. **Move forward by not thinking (unless you really
have to)** – This statement often appears as an

unintelligent remark; however, by close examination you will understand how powerful this message actually is. What is suggested here is that you can discipline yourself to <u>think at will</u> and only allow the pending thoughts to progress if you and only you have already established a desired outcome from your thought process and you have reasonable confidence that you can get to a helpful answer. If with the best of intentions, you fail getting the final answers, your pursuit is not wasted and can form a solid platform for your subsequent explorations.

Before you commence with your topic of thought, ask yourself, "If I am going to spend "X" amount of time thinking about "Y", am I going to have something of value at the end of my thinking process that can help me to achieve "Z" in my life? If the answer is **NO**, immediately stop your thinking process. Ensure that you do not waste your precious time and energy for only revivifying unimportant/ head produced dramas on a continuous basis that you consciously know do not serve you at all, and on the contrary encourage negative feelings and bitterness within you. If you think about the actual amount of time we really need for our conscious thinking activities, you may be surprised to learn how little time we actually require on a given day to day basis to think. Unless your job necessitates you to think, please <u>stop thinking</u> and when you are meant to think, ensure you get something decent and productive out of it. In other words – why waste so much time and energy for getting nowhere or at worst, end up with less value than what you started with (having additional negativities and stresses)?

For example, if I am thinking about what I should have for dinner tonight, even though it is a simple thought, it is a good thought and I should allow it to progress as it would eventually lead to a clear final decision on what to eat tonight. On the other hand, if my mind is gravitating towards a concept of bitterness about someone who may have upset me in some way, this type of thinking may not produce any real resolution for me, even if I spend hours repeating in my head and saying things like 'why did she say that and why did I do that'. As soon as such thoughts begin to manifest, I should quickly and consciously stop them by saying to the inner voice 'are you going to give me anything of substance when I finish with you?' and if the answer is NO, then I must drop such thoughts immediately as they do not pay off, even though my grieved subconscious mind is dying for me to go back and forth regurgitating the negativity for hours to no avail.

ALWAYS look for solutions rather than waste your energy crying over spilt milk.

4. **Develop higher dimensions for searching, thinking and acting** – Your general interest in knowing and questioning the big picture of life and the universe will undoubtedly open opportunities for you to more broadly examine your life within such a wider context that can subsequently reduce the chance of dramatization and projection of your subjective experiences into your awareness. Similar to a storm in a tea cup.

Try to appreciate the sense of oneness/ coherence in all things and always value the contribution and need of all life constituents. This can open up a new dimension of wisdom within you and influence your daily perception of events and your corresponding behaviour.

The more holistically you look at life and understand it, the less you worry or become trapped in the silos of your thoughts. In a wide and varied way learn about all aspects of life, investigate different philosophies and question everything from your childhood adoption of various rules and beliefs all the way to your recent indoctrination of any negative or rigid behaviour. Realise all pains and sorrows begin in your mind and they manifest in your body (impact on the state of health and beauty) and all other external bodies and objects in order to form and materialise your subjective reality.

The obvious example of this could be witnessed in the state of mental perspective, behaviour and actions of a wide range of people in society. At one end of the spectrum, you could imagine people who have no interest in the big picture of life (silo focused) who are constantly engaged and preoccupied with the day-to-day dramas of life with lots of issues and worries about what confronts them. They may see their issues from a limited subjective perspective, feel highly stressed for their inability to change things for the better and mostly feel unfulfilled. At the other end of the spectrum, you could imagine certain people who are constantly searching for answers to the mysteries of life and the universe. They aspire to have peace and harmony in life instead of pain and suffering. They want to know why they are here and question their purpose within the context of the systemic universe. Such individuals could be confronted with exactly the same issues and challenges in life and yet, they suffer less stress and are driven to be more connected, remain conscious and live to learn.

5. **Understand how the mind works** – In continuing your effort for greater understanding of the forces around you, joyfully, become a high level expert in how the human mind works. It is quite easy to learn. All you require is your passion for knowing the essence of who you actually are and how you think and behave. Understanding the self can provide the necessary base for you to question your negative ways and consciously change your

inner in order to bring about and maintain your quality of life on the outer.

Have you ever thought why so many people have this serious aversion and deliberately avoid knowing about the characteristics of what goes on in their minds and in their lives? This could be due to the unnoticeable/ subtle dominant nature of the subconscious over the conscious mind, especially when an individual is not generally familiar with how to exercise "conscious will" over the emotionally charged experiences. Such individuals with a disempowered conscious mind would also find it hard to sit still, relax and meditate as their subconscious hates to lose its control.

6. **Notice any small internal movements within you** – Become more sensitive to your internal voice and the interactions between the Conscious and Subconscious minds (who is saying what to whom and why). Notice the emotion as it rises and learn about the type of pressures the subconscious places on the Conscious. Say to yourself, 'I am noticing this internal dialogue' and here we go again and watch the interactions. Ensure you DO NOT get caught in your feelings and just remain as an observer.

This is a somewhat alien concept for most people to comprehend and practice. The easiest way to realise is to note that there are <u>two of you</u> in your head. For example, when you talk to yourself, it implies there must be two parties present (talker and listener) otherwise, no conversation could possibly take place. The notion of this identification opens amazing new possibilities and soul searching such as:

- Who is talking to whom and which one is the real me?
- Which one is the wiser one?
- Who is the controlling one?
- Which one should I really trust?
- What are the mandates and driving forces for each of these two minds?
- What should they want from one another?
- Are they part of the same system serving the same master?
- If they have different masters, how come they belong to the same organisation/ system?

With genuine intention and conscious practice, you learn to wake up from the dual nature of your mind and see the two aspects working within you.

7. **Get in touch with your inner hidden drivers and beliefs** – In my view this is the main reason why we are born into this life – "to resolve all leftover and unhealthy views on life that are currently shaping us with our current energy fields of attraction and repulsion". We owe it to ourselves to consciously roll our sleeves up and get to work. We need to expand on the knowledge of our systemic universe to allow the emergence of new insights that can allow our individual inner tapestry to be openly displayed

and reveal our true purpose of being. This soul searching endeavour will fill in the missing link aspect of our place in the universe, change our perspectives and bring a sense of purpose into our lives. It helps us answer the question of who we are and what we are made up of, what we are to do and why?

Our combined hard and soft core intelligence allows us to survive, learn and develop objects to sustain us individually and collectively as social entities. There are many combinations of concepts and things we can perform in life. The question you need to ask yourself is 'why do I end up having this set of understanding, aspiration, behaviours and experiences which are so different to anyone else around me'? What is it that uniquely defines me and decides I should do this and that?

The more we question the roots of our foundations, the more we can change the underlying beliefs and drivers for a better and wiser existence. We can consciously help ourselves, or even get external help from holistic practitioners and address all the underlying beliefs that are not in line with our greater good and harmony in life. Do not become slaves to the obsessive fuelled drivers as they become your masters and rob you from the potential for a peaceful existence.

8. **Realise you can choose to be happy** – Consciously and honestly ask yourself 'if I had a real choice in my life, would I rather be happy or sad'? Remember

at any moment in time, you can be happy or sad, or somewhere in between. Despite what happens in front of you, you could choose to feel OK. There is absolutely no gain in being miserable. If you disagree, please write down the benefits of being miserable and read it out to yourself or even better, go public with it. You can imagine two people in an exact situation responding differently to the same event. For example, they could have both lost their jobs in an exact circumstance, but one is cool about it and looks at new opportunities and the other person is angry, revengeful, and sad or perhaps a touch suicidal. The point here is not about being happy when you lose your job, it is about the concept that your real happiness is not dependent on the fact that everything has to go your way or else. A bit of wisdom could reveal that life takes us down different paths and changes our world constantly, we could just appreciate the journey and smile as we go through it. The reason we feel miserable is because our emotional mind (the sub-conscious) generates the sad emotional response in accordance with its rigid and sometimes false expectations of life. Ask yourself, "Do I REALLY want to be happy"? If the answer is "YES" then, next time your subconscious whispers in your ear to be sad or miserable, you consciously allow yourself to intervene and say "my state of being is not dependent on my subconscious emotional ups and downs and for this reason, I choose to be happy, relaxed and follow my passion for new adventures". Every time you challenge your subconscious mind, you regain more and more conscious powers and freedom from dramas and potential preoccupation with negativities.

Our deep personal cravings for living a happy life and experiencing a quality of life on a sustainable basis (in terms of physical and mental wellbeing) <u>can only be achieved</u> when our conscious vigilance rises to a level that we can: 1) consciously override our emotional biases; 2) easily change our redundant beliefs at will and: 3) recognise the context of the systemic nature of our world and its dynamic influences.

How to Change Beliefs

Human Potential for Change

To create opportunities for us to change for the better, we first need to genuinely believe and fully embrace the following:

> <u>If you believe in them, please adopt them,</u>
> <u>live them fully and see the miracles.</u>

1. The facts are – all humans have the basic ingredients and capacity for re-evaluating and fine tuning their lives for the better.

2. As an individual's conscious awareness rises through exposure to new insights and perspectives, the person's quality of intelligence

will also evolve organically and as the quality of the intelligence increases, in a direct correlation to the quality of their life which shall also increase.

3. Basically, the more we consciously know and become aware of what the beliefs that drive us every moment of our lives are, the more we can objectively assess them; refine them so their potential emotional sting does not cloud our day-to-day objectivity and the assessment of our situation in life.

4. This awareness will allow us to make better decisions and consequently improve the quality of our lives.

5. Disregarding the challenges presented in our immediate environment and individual situations, the quality of our intelligence can really make us to stand out and shine. It makes us shine in the way we consciously select the possible options in life that can finally lead us towards the best possible scenario in our given circumstance.

6. The greatest gift to humanity is their innate aspiration for greater knowledge and their objective awareness of their present reality. This is in view of how an individual can perceive the world, interpret it and respond to it in order to establish and maintain his/ her sustainable quality of life.

Incentives to Change Beliefs

For any change to take place, we generally require real incentives and opportunities before we can initiate the change process. Therefore to understand how to change beliefs, first we must understand how we can find incentives in life. The best reason to change is when we realise that we can do better than we are currently doing and consciously drive ourselves to change our beliefs. Sometimes life pushes us hard towards the edge in spite of our general human reluctance to change, we have no choice but to embrace change.

The Circle of Change (*designed by Soltani Therapy*)

The Circle of Change is about how we may change our current ways.

Change Your Life ← Change Your Mind ← Change Your Beliefs ← Change Your Resistance ← Understand Life Diversities ← Choose To be Conscious

Why change at all?

The reason we change anything in life is because we can see compelling reasons to do something different to the normal way and also as we realise that our current position is no longer serving us well, we recognise new ways required to deal with our changing environment and circumstances. The intention for adopting change is always to better one's current situation. The general personal response to our changing environment means that we are consciously trying to assimilate change in our lives the best way we know.

What is it we want to change?

In general, we change things in order to protect what matters to us. Ultimately most desires we currently have directly point to the quality of life which we would like to satisfy/ preserve. We see our individual quality of life to include whatever we perceive to be appropriate for us. For example, you may view the health and happiness of your children as the most important thing to you or you may adopt a more universal view for the health and wellbeing of humanity at large. It could be materially based or spiritually driven. Remember, we change things only to maintain and preserve our quality of life. Otherwise why bother to change if the subject does not matter to us.

Why change our minds?

So if the quality of our life is what we would like to preserve, the only way to improve it is by doing something better or different from our current thinking and practices. So our mind, in terms of its overall potential for perceiving, rationalising and acting, has to change. Basically we need to change our mind in order to have any chance of improving the quality of our lives.

Why change our beliefs?

In order to change the mind, to think and act differently, first we need to change the fundamental beliefs supporting its current way. This means that we can view our beliefs, for whatever they represent, only as potential (not an absolute state) and the ones we are currently holding could be changed or refined to reflect a more realistic version of life's reality and its governing rules. No matter how much we rely on our beliefs as the true representation of our reality, by definition, we must mercilessly reject the opposite view. Therefore in such a paradigm, the potential for change in our current beliefs become a small possibility. We all possess a human tendency that subconsciously gravitates us to remain as we currently are (undisturbed) and hope that the world will change around us while we are standing still and holding to our established way.

Why change resistance?

The reason we hang on to our current beliefs (what we know) is due to our resistance to seek any alternatives as potential options. We tend to reject the unfamiliar and radical beliefs in place of what we currently know and feel comfortable with. How do we actually know what we believe to be true is actually true, unless we can openly and unbiasedly examine the opposition. The art of being able to float between polarities and appreciate the two sidedness of everything is a great virtue. Once we expose our conscious vigilance to a more open and unbiased perspective, better chance we create for ourselves to have a well-rounded understanding of what we are dealing with and how we should intelligently respond to what is happening around us.

<u>Why do we need to understand life diversities?</u>

If we recognise that through diversity we are able to learn and grow, we can actively develop more flexibility and an appetite for considering other views and perspectives with the kind of respect that each deserve. To appreciate the importance of diversity in our lives, we need to realise the entire concept of existence rests on the world of duality and the recognition of the two opposing sides can make us stronger in our knowledge and wisdom. The tree of knowledge is about knowing the opposing views and not just focusing on one side. Of course we always end up making decisions on what we need to do in life, but it is best that we are more informed from wider perspectives.

Why choose to be Conscious?

In order to lose our resistance to diversity, we need to move away from the world of duality and see people and the world form the position of the creator and oneness. As much as possible, we need to remain untouched by the influences of our subconscious beliefs and recognise the position and importance of everyone and everything in this amazing universe.

13.

Defining the vision for a new intelligent world

Preparation and mind-set adjustments

The following paragraphs are to help us prepare and adjust our current perspectives for future social change.

Entertaining the Idea of personal and social Freedom

I suppose the first question is, as a human race do we deserve to live in peace and harmony, be given the appropriate nurturing opportunities and social support to equitably and sustainably enjoy and prosper together in life? Is there anybody who may disagree with such ideas?

Obviously the concept of visualising the possibility of such a new social order, which is peaceful and civilised, is totally foreign to most of us, because, as the human race, we have never experienced global social justice, true human collaboration or harmony. There is always some group in society losing out and losing out badly. History is always about never ending global issues relating to cruelty, social deprivation and ignorant attitudes.

Let's be honest, none of us are really used to imagining our world could possibly operate humanely, intelligently and with inclusive rights of all of its inhabitants. Could we?

> If you assume that there is no hope, you guarantee that there will be no hope. If you assume that there is an instinct for freedom, that there are opportunities to change things, then there is a possibility that you can contribute to making a better world.
> **—Noam Chomsky**

Changing our deceptive perception of being innately barbaric

We have been socially manipulated to believe that wickedness, violence and wars are unavoidable in our society. We have been told due to our competitive and greedy human nature, it is just unavoidable for us to simply be loving, caring, collaborative and share life in harmony. Such statements are of course far from the truth. According to many eminent psychologists and social scientists, it is actually in our genes, to be more harmonious, loving and sympathetic than competitive, cruel or selfish.

Unfortunately we have generally accepted the current state of chaos and unavoidable human suffering as how things just are in this world. So we often feel powerless and we say to ourselves, what can we do? We just resign, accept and live with such nastiness as we are made to believe is our human fate. How did we buy such rubbish from our social manipulators?

How is this possible? How can an incredibly small minority, who are sadly morally bankrupt and spiritually less gifted than the rest of us, easily influence and win over the masses, the ordinary people? I strongly argue that we collectively need to wake up and start believing in our inherent good nature as a loving and caring species. We should refuse the lies that have been told by our social manipulators that we are barbaric by nature so we deserve to endure our present social chaos and accept our sealed human fate.

Watch for subliminal Social messages

As a clinical practitioner, I can't help, but notice the clever and elaborate disguises often used by certain groups to guide humanity into a predestined direction. Unless you deliberately look for these disguises, you would not see them or realise how these intentional subliminal messages are controlling our daily lives.

Such mind manipulation techniques include subtle suggestions and auto-suggestions in order to convince us how we should interpret what we witness and how we should think. If we observe carefully, we can notice them all around us in various staged propagandas, suggestive publications and the passage of misinformation through official media.

Stretch our vision and explore new possibilities

For these self-defeating socially engineered reasons, if we are going to imagine new social possibilities for ourselves, we need to truly stretch ourselves and come out of our limiting and restrictive social costumes. Maybe we can dust off our dormant, but free spirited creative imagination and allow ourselves to go well beyond our current social mind-sets and the way the majority of us have been indoctrinated by our limited social visions and possibilities. We must by pass the fairy tales we have been told by some shady social engineers to legitimise their agendas for social divisions, the creation of untold human sufferings and wars.

Remember if we hesitate to think freely or fail to initiate and set things right in our existing failed civilisation, who else do you honestly think is going to do it for us? Do you seriously believe our current leaders, who are still living within the limitations of their failed political and social paradigms, are going to help us? Those leaders who have been upholding their outdated social frameworks and ignorantly delivering our current state of chaos for as long as we can remember? Those who have been persistently failing to create a civilised world for our global social system. Those who keep on failing to think intelligently and act systemically in order to eradicate our local and global social miseries? No I don't think it is a good idea to go to our leaders for real advice on how to create a better society.

All political ideologies are by definition limited by nature as each one can only represent a static or fixed perspective on our overall or emerging social challenges. The only social ideology that should faithfully be upheld is the preservation of the Human Bill of Rights. All political decisions should be purely based on intelligent analysis and the fit for purpose approach to our social challenges rather than the current narrow minded political ideologies. It is moronic to think that as an advanced race of the 21st century, we are still stuck with backward current politicians who always hide behind their party's ideologies rather than intelligently tackling our social problems with holistic vision and unreserved consideration to our Human Bill of Rights.

For your information, many supposedly advanced countries such as Australia do not even have a clearly defined set of Human Bill of Rights (a single constitutional document) for their people. Somehow the ruling politicians do not see such luxuries as relevant to the people they are meant to serve and protect.

> No fundamental social change occurs merely because a government acts. It's because civil society, the conscience of a country, begins to rise up and demand – demand – demand change.
>
> **—Joe Biden**

If you look at it logically, you notice there is no confusion here. Our global and international communities never had it so good in terms of our scientific nous and technological capability and yet our leaders who are supposed to be managing the social world of coexistence are somehow depriving humanity from its basic rights and its social entitlement for peace and harmony.

OK, to define our new beautiful social paradigm, let's first define and put a framework around what we mean by civilised human existence before we focus on how we may achieve this.

How can we create a holistic and nurturing social structure for humanity?

What are the steps for reinventing ourselves for the better?

In order to create a clever design and establish a lasting social change for our civilised society, we need to first define a logical and workable framework. The following points are to help provide us with the required steps for ensuring a successful journey for change:

1. Define what human and social needs are and what we need to consider and satisfy in our newly designed systemic structure. This should be relatively easy, because we all have an understanding of what these needs are;

2. Investigate how these requirements can translate into the design of our new civilised world and explore how it can work and what it looks like on a day-to-day basis. How it can operate viably and be successful on an ongoing basis;

3. Demonstrate the advantages of this new system over our crippled current social system that we collectively agree has passed its use by date and is totally dysfunctional;

4. Describe what resources and capabilities are required in order for such a social structure to operate effectively, fairly and sustainably;

5. How realistic is it to achieve such a new social vision both from the scientific and social perspective.

Defining what Civilised Human Social Existence means
What do we mean by a <u>Civilised Human Social Existence</u>? Of course there are many ways people may think about what 'civilised human existence' might mean, but for the sake of our exercise, I give the following explanation of how I see the boundaries of a civilised human existence:

- Firstly, when we, as social members, can collectively begin to truly take stock, measure and appreciate the **role**, the **place** and the **worth** of what currently exists in our world (i.e. people, animals, plants and resources within our ecosystem). Basically appreciating what significance and roles these entities signify to us as a society. Put them in some order and definition.

- Secondly, through such understanding, as a society, we learn how we should treat everyone and everything with reverence and deal with them in accordance to their systemic presence, place and values.

The acknowledgement of the presence of the sense of divinity in all living beings means that we consciously become:

- First interested in the true needs of people, animals and plants that are in fact, the main constituents of this planet, then,

- We begin to intelligently and eagerly become interested in understanding how everything interacts together, where everything is placed in our ecosystem and how their potential value (the potential value of people, animal and other objects) can be tapped/ harnessed, allow them to manifest and deliver systemic benefits to people and the world at large.

Every one of us possesses amazing latent potential that can only be realised under the right circumstances and environment. I am sure many of us have been frustrated in the past when our potential has been dismissed or ignored by others or the system that narrowly misunderstand us.

These basic realisations can give us so many clues on how we may define our civilised paradigm.

In summary, we need to regard everyone and everything around us intelligently with wider perspectives and greater recognition of what they actually mean to us and to our dynamic ecosystem. Through such understanding, we then consciously start to treat everyone and everything with total respect for what they represent in our systemic world (i.e. we look at their systemic presence, place and value). For example; killing innocent creatures, large and small is purely ignorant, such as killing a spider because we, being 1 million times bigger, are scared of them). Please stop killing or alienating things that you don't like through lack of understanding.

Basically our systemic world teaches us to be nice to one another, because logically it make sense. I am not talking about the spiritual or religious concept of what we are often taught about love thy neighbour. I am saying that Intelligence alone tells us we are better off by systemically caring for one another and working harmoniously with one another than hating each other or competing against one another. Basically, we prosper more in the long term by being humane.

The definition of a new set of world-wide human Principles & Practices

What are the human and social needs that should be addressed and satisfied by such a newly designed systemic structure? The first thing we need to establish before anything else, is to collectively, locally and internationally define and sum up what we <u>mean and want</u> as our human rights, human needs and human values.

We can regard this newly defined set of requirements as the <u>**Sacrosanct Human Principles**</u>.

These principles are incredibly important, as we shall shortly learn how these human principles will literally drive the way we, the human race, will <u>individually and collectively</u> live and act in our newly defined civilised world. We will also be measuring and holding our governments and businesses accountable for their diligent adherence and social execution of these principles. These principles will become our true foundation and provide the framework for how anything will be done in our civilisation.

We need to create an appropriate social engagement process and invite public views in order to collectively define these fundamental principles and get them endorsed.

For example, from my personal perspective, I can think of four commonly understood principles that most civilised human beings may agree with:

Principle-1: Human Unity – According to this principle, we as a human race will view and regard every soul on this planet as a divine and worthy aspect of creation. We need to view everyone as a unique individual with legitimate rights to exist, to be honoured, respected and supported by society.

We truly need to regard people as our families, brothers or sisters. To me this principle is as civilised as we can ever get as a human race, just for simply honouring and acknowledging the place and significance of everyone in our society.

> He who experiences the unity of life, sees his
> own Self in all beings, all beings in his own.
>
> **—Buddha**

If you could imagine our social body (the macro body) to comprise of our family members, community, work, country or our international body. we could also visualise people as small cells inside such a social macro body.

Now visualise yourself as merely a single cell, a very small cell living amongst many other cells (other people) and working closely with your neighbour cells (people you deal with in life) and you interact with everyone in order to provide for the bigger body that you belong to (community, country, the world).

Just like the way you expect a healthy cell in your body to work and engage with other cells harmoniously and cooperatively in order for your body to function at its peak. Therefore you would intelligently and logically expect that your cells should behave and work harmoniously with each other and ideally not kill each other or refuse to share food with other cells. You don't expect your cells to derail your healthy body by their petty and internal struggles.

When we have internal struggles amongst our cells, it means that our body is getting sick. We know that when parts within us are fighting one another.

This is exactly why our current society is very sick, because there are constant feuds amongst its members (its cells) that are tearing its social body apart. We have a very sick society that is profusely haemorrhaging unnecessarily.

Imagine you are a small cell and are working purposefully in order to allow the overall body to prosper and function well, because your intelligence tells you that your livelihood directly depends on the bigger body's livelihood. If other cells in your body die due to mismanagement, as a healthy cell in that body, you will also die due to your failing environment.

Now since we can imagine such affinity with our macro or bigger world, we should ideally, think and act to support the bigger cause and ensure the body you are meant to serve is taken care of effectively. We must make sure the overall body (our society) possesses enduring health and receives abundant material goodies necessary for its survival and nurturing purposes. We must make sure every cell/ member in that body receives from the systemic world that it belongs to.

For these reasons we should work harmoniously with others around us in order to help the bigger system (the society and beyond) to function properly and by doing so, we will feel purposeful and complete in our lives.

At the same time, your action and your contribution also allows the systemic change to take place in your holographic image of life. This picture has the same presence, look and feel as many possible or imagined dimensions covering the entire spectrum of our macro and micro worlds. They all look the same, just like Russian dolls.

Basically by serving humanity, we serve the bigger system and in the process we shall receive well-earned material prosperity so we can less focus on our day to day survival needs and put our main attention on our purposeful creative self and manifest out values and help humanity through our art and passion. This systemic clue teaches us that the more we caringly live with one another, the more we collectively prosper.

Under the principle of Human Unity, the concept of competition is totally discouraged as it causes imbalances in the system; basically competition rewards some handsomely at the expense of not meeting the needs of the larger system. The concept of two cells competing in the same body is not good for the body. Is it? It means that the body (the society) loses at the end and also systemically speaking, competition does not serve any real value to the masses. Instead of competing, if two cells collaborate with one another, their collective powers become much larger than sum total of their individual ones.

From time to time, you may hear some say that if we don't have to compete, we become stagnant, lazy and our level of effectiveness and motivation will drop significantly.

Of course these ideas are totally untrue and have managed to fool people for a long time. Such ideas will keep encouraging humanity to compete with one other in total ignorance of the power of unity. We must realise that through our new social reform, once our fears for survival have disappeared, there will be no reason to compete any longer and we will individually become more creative and collaborative in our daily and life pursuits.

Once the competition disappears in our work places and our communities, people naturally become more creative, spontaneous and amazingly productive and contribute through personal choice and not through social pressure.

In summary, the great meaning behind the principle of Human Unity or oneness is that it allows us to understand why we need to be loving and caring for one another and how we must live together like brothers and sisters and creatively serve the larger humanity.

There are logical, intelligent and systemic reasons why we need to be united as a race and how such practices can bring real prosperity to humanity. Of course we can discuss and concur amongst ourselves how such collective collaborations, mutual interactions and purposeful unity can serve greater good for humanity.

Priniciple-2: <u>Human Equality</u> – According to this principle, all human beings of any colour, shape, size or belief can receive an <u>equal amount and quality of</u> food, shelter, life opportunities, protection, education and health care.

This means disregarding what social station you have in life, for example, a CEO, professor, a fisherman or a tea boy, you would receive the same amount and the <u>same quality</u> of food, shelter, health care and access to education as any other person in your society.

In other words, no one is regarded as more preferential to anybody else because of their station or level of influence in life.

> True equality means holding everyone accountable in the same way, regardless of race, gender, faith, ethnicity – or political ideology.
>
> **—Monica Crowley**

This principle will fairly and squarely separate the civilised practices from the cruel barbarian's practices which by nature create social imbalances and inequalities. I am sure none of you civilised people would enjoy eating lavish food in the comfort of your mansion, while watching hordes of innocent children and families dying of malnutrition outside your gates.

To me such disparities are the ingredients for a very sick and badly managed society and it is a sad indication of uncivilised human practices.

The Human Equality principle will establish the corner stone for what it really means to be truly civilised. This will remove our current level of imbalance between rich and poor that is currently paralysing our world on its knees.

Principle-3: <u>Rights of Animals, Plants & Environment (APE) rights</u> – all animal lives, plant lives and our environment are to be respected and subjected to fair treatment and tolerance of our ecosystem. Therefore, we need to re-examine our unstainable consumerist society and abandon products that either are inhumane or do not serve us holistically or are produced at the expense of our precious environment. If you closely examine the usefulness of a variety of products we innocently purchase on a daily basis, you may notice how much we are psychologically and continuously influenced by marketers to purchase objects we don't necessarily need in life. We need to learn to appreciate life not just through what we possess, but through our conscious human experiences, contributions and interactions.

> There is massive propaganda for everyone to consume. Consumption is good for profits and consumption is good for the political establishment.
>
> **—Noam Chomsky**

Principle-4: Ecosystem Sustainability – all decisions and actions have to honour the concept of sustainability and take into account the ramifications of actions on humanity, animals, plants and environment.

All decisions should carefully consider and weigh up the causal and the dynamic relationship between the players. We need to holistically and consciously minimise any adverse impact on the players and constituents of the ecosystem (which is people, animal, plant and environment).

Therefore no monetary values should ever be placed on the provision and application of goods and services to meet human basic needs. For example, the pharmaceutical companies will purely exist in future to deliver value to humanity and financial gains are no longer the drivers. The only important thing for them is how to sustainably deliver value to people. It means that we build cars, houses and infrastructure goods, purely to serve humanity and not just to make big profits and compromise on the quality, value and suitability of products.

For example, under such a value based principle, no authority or individuals can ever derive at a decision or action that could result in human cruelties or unfair human practices as the above 3 principles collectively will not allow such a shortfall to occur in our new intelligent society.

14.

Organic Implementation of the New Social Paradigm

Our greatest asset in social reformation is our concept of <u>Human Principles</u>. Once it is defined and becomes accepted by the people, it becomes our magical tool for reshaping the world. Under such a strategy, we don't transform the world overnight as the change burden would be too brutal on many in our society. Our key to success is based on the specific application of organic means. In my view, the Human Principles are the necessary instrument for social change and they can directly enable our organic journey to successfully triumph.

The implementation of the new social paradigm has to be carefully carried out through the evolution of viable social concepts. It has to be intelligently executed to ensure ongoing sustainable outcomes. For the sake of applying intelligence, our implementation <u>cannot</u> be about a violent uprising or starting a war against anyone. <u>Definitely Not</u>. It must be based on uniting rather than dividing people.

An eye for an eye only ends up making the whole world blind.

—Mahatma Gandhi

Our action should simply be about claiming the consistent delivery of legitimate human rights and entitlements from local and international official governing bodies. By using our electoral rights, we can demand the official bodies allow us to collectively and sustainably live and prosper in a harmoniously structured society.

As a deserving human race, we need to stand firm together with unshakable united determination in order to achieve peaceful outcomes. In this implementation there will be <u>no witch hunts</u> of the Self-Serving ones or any other oppressing entities as this kind of action will not be in line with our ideal future social harmony. The global adoption of our newly defined set of human principles will automatically readjust all the current unfair practices across government, corporations and general social arenas to behave responsibly.

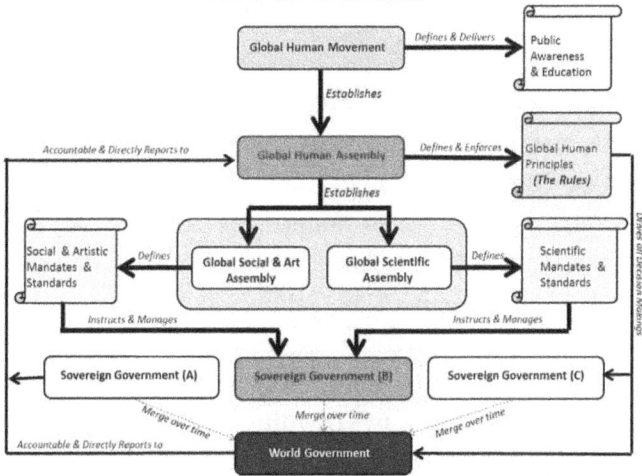

New Social Architecture

The greatest Challenge for us to Overcome

It is important to note the Self-Serving class possesses a highly sophisticated network of global influence and mind controlling capabilities that have been refined and made potently effective over many centuries. They have successfully survived many human revolts for justice throughout history. Their cleverness and manipulative powers should never be underestimated.

There is no doubt there will be massive opposition and backlash by the Self-Serving class to derail any future human movements toward fairer social reforms. However, the wishes of the majority should ultimately prevail as the Self-Serving class cannot openly stand against mass human demands for a fairer society.

So how can our peaceful movement proceed forward and succeed in view of such a powerful adversary?

Understanding the Self-Serving class methods of manipulation

In order to have an upper hand over the Self-Serving ones, first we need to understand how their manipulative techniques are actually deployed and publically implemented. Remember they have all the money, resources and power to manipulate humanity as they please. They basically keep people in the dark either by depriving them of available information or they provide misinformation to misconstrue the truth and manufacture psychological lies, legitimise their inhumane agendas by dividing society and often blaming the innocents. In the worst case scenario, whenever their manipulation techniques fail, they use brute force through deployment of their controlled law enforcement arms such as police or military to quash any civil movements for justice. Please note the majority of people serving in the police or army are totally innocent. In their minds, they are actually serving the public by maintaining social order and restoring civil obedience. It is not them, but the actual system that is corrupt at its highest levels.

The Self-Serving class clearly understand that people naturally respond to the concept of 'threat or opportunity'. They know through our fears, we can create mental borders, social borders and national borders to keep those who we consider a threat out of our immediate surroundings or jurisdiction. They use this concept effectively to make people fear each other's race, beliefs, culture or religion. They divide communities, nations and encourage people to turn against one another on the fictitious basis of 'us and them'. Unless they can fallaciously demonstrate that there are impending threats out there for us to fear, it is impossible for them to mobilise people against one another. With every lie, they create more public fears and through fears, bit by bit, they openly and without any shame take away our human rights and privacy.

> The more you can increase fear of drugs, crime, welfare mothers, immigrants and aliens, the more you control all of the people.
>
> **—Noam Chomsky**

In summary, through its selected powerful minions, the Self-Serving class can maintain its total grip on power almost indefinitely. They can artfully deceive, psychologically manipulate the public and defeat all challenges against themselves. Their main instruments for success are their controlled official media and the government allies that publically legitimise their clandestine intentions.

How to minimise the global influence of the Self-Serving class

- So for our peaceful social movement to succeed, we need to be more organised and successful in networking and sharing with others what we understand to be true in our world.

- Since we are all socially conditioned to heavily rely on what is generally presented to us by our official media on our TV or computer screens as the only version of truth, we need to consciously learn to change such dangerous habits and use alternative channels and media for our wider exposure to what is taking place around us in this world;

- One thing that goes in our favour is that all our official governing bodies, almost always, gloss and promote themselves to their constituencies as socially conscious, caring and just. They never say that they are going to be cruel, unfair and mainly serve the Corporatocracy. We need to capitalise on this empty political gesture and hold our leaders accountable. Now time has come to hold them to their promises or even better, we, the people can give a list of what we expect them to deliver if they want to stay in office.

- To effectively change our crippled political scene, we all need to become politically active and have a say in our social affairs. We also need to constantly stay vigilant and expose those leaders who are just serving themselves by serving their Corporatocracy masters rather than their electorates.

- We need to learn to recognise and stop being scared by the socially manufactured threats, refuse to allow them to divide our society and alienate innocent people by labelling them as 'them – the adversaries'. Remember an occurrence of a cruel social mayhem, is almost always intended to satisfy and legitimise a secretive agenda of a faceless Self-Serving entity.

- We need to always remind ourselves that we (humanity at large) are not barbaric, not naturally cruel and certainly do not consciously seek injustice. Therefore we should not fear each other, ignorantly embrace our official lies that exaggerate and deliberately demonise our differences.

- We need to become more tolerant of some people who may at times act in selfish, cruel or racist ways. We need to realise that such people are innocently conditioned and socially manipulated to think and act like they do. Remember we need to help educate, wake each other up and assist everyone to see the truth around ourselves rather than point fingers at others.

Establishing a New Peaceful Human Movement

This will require great leadership from a handful of committed, influential and balanced individuals who believe that people have the right, legitimacy and capability to start a new global human movement for establishing an equitable and sustainable social

structure for all to enjoy. This is NOT A REVOLU-
TION against our governments. It is purely about
creating a sense of clarity of what we collectively want
from our governments. Basically, we need to perceive
our governments as our service providers and we (the
citizens) need to have a consensus and views on what
we collectively expect from them, how we wish to
measure them and sack them if they are not delivering
value. All we need to do is to collectively become politically involved and express our free views openly
about how social decisions are made on our behalf.

There will be a great need for this movement to sign
up and increase the number of its followers through the
effective promotion of its proposed future social possibilities. The effective propagation of the awareness
raising information can be significantly aided through
effective use of the available social media and also via
relevant targeted public presentations. It is essential
for this movement to gather the necessary momentum
for establishing its credible social presence, and public
recognition of its legitimacy as a united global group.
In order to start our journey of social reform, we
need to take the first step and create a small hub of
committed and peacefully energised individuals at its
centre and it will grow fast and reach the entire world
population.

No governments can openly oppose such a peaceful
body as the sentiments behind the movement are
exactly what they (governments) are meant to deliver
to their citizens in the first place. With the exception

of some backward international political thinkers who don't see eye to eye with the Human Rights movement (such as certain rulers who shamelessly and publically advocate social brutality), most governments will not have the nerve to openly stand and say they are against human rights and values.

The Human Global Movement can soon begin to challenge the current established political mind sets and give the officials reasons to think hard about their arcane political practices and general excuses for mishandling important social agendas by shamelessly favouring their Self-Serving masters.

The primary reason why the world is the way it is may be due to general human apathy, lack of interest to stand up, have a voice and be counted as socially aware and participating individuals. For this reason the ruling class has had it really easy and continued to treat people like fools and generally get away with their ongoing manipulations. As we all know, it really does not matter which political party is in power, the overall result is more or less the same. Because the Self-Serving class's objectives are always effectively served by the powers exercised through their established arm of corporatocracy (the movers and shakers of this world). They cleverly lobby, fund and ultimately influence the elected party of the day for how to set favourable political agendas and how to carry them out.

The challenge of overcoming human apathy to effectively participate in social reforms is even more pronounced in the west than other parts of the world where people are often directly forced to wake up and become more socially and politically active due to their oppressive social and political upheavals. The people in the west are relatively more cocooned and sheltered from direct day-to-day serious hardships that are often experienced by nations in social turmoil.

This does not mean that people in the west are uncaring or cruel. It means that they are potentially desensitised through their official brain washing media or they are just simply so busy and preoccupied with their day to day activities and unreasonable engineered social pressures that they end up having no time or energy to concern themselves with the wider social issues and injustices. They have got plenty of their own to deal with first.

This is quite an alarming phenomenon that many people just don't really care how they are governed or question the consequences of the decisions made by the officials on their behalf. The majority of people just want to be left alone, sometimes they are so traumatised in their lives that they just want to lick their wounds in their little private world and expect all their social issues to hopefully be taken care of by the authorities. They generally absolve themselves from all responsibility for being involved in any social decision making process. For this reason, it suits the masses, to innocently adopt the herd mentality and just simply go along with whatever authorities tell them and unless something really awful happens that may directly impact them, they are happy to wash their hands totally of politics or how things may be run on their behalf.

> One of the penalties for refusing to participate in politics is that you end up being governed by your inferiors.
>
> **—Plato**

Therefore the challenge for the new social reform greatly rests on how effectively it can wake up the masses, get their undivided attention and shift their mind set from apathy to direct participation in their social affairs. In my opinion, the greatest tool for such an awareness-raising process is the provision of wide spread exposure and education through all available alternative medias.

> Most humans live their lives in a state of hypnotic "waking sleep", but that it is possible to transcend to a higher state of consciousness and achieve full human potential.
>
> **—G.I Gurdjieff**

This book amongst many other publications can be a good place to start. The main job of the Global Human Movement is just to wake people up and allow them to intelligently see their current social realities and make them understand their future potential for positive social change.

Education is the most powerful weapon
which you can use to change the world.
—Nelson Mandela

Creation of the Global Human Assembly

It sounds a bit like a name from the Star War movies. The idea behind this assembly is to create a visible global human presence that can become the voice of the civilised human race.

Once the Global Human Movement has reached a respectable and influential position in its journey of social recognition, as a matter of priority, this peak assembly must be established. The main role of the assembly is to represent people's collective needs and wishes as a race for the entire world. There will also be a need to create sub representative satellite bodies in every country, city, town and village representing the sentiments and essence of humanity through its Global Social and Artistic Assembly arm (defined below). At some future point, this assembly will become the overall authority for humanity and all future governments of the world will only exist to serve the wishes of such a global body. All governments will be answerable and accountable to this body for all their day-to-day decision making processes and actions.

Why do we need such an assembly? If we logically examine how our political machinery is structured in most sovereign countries, we will notice there is always a glaring vacuum between where ordinary people reside and how removed their representative governments are from them. Since people are generally not collectively organised and do not unitedly articulate what their needs and expectations are from their society, they haphazardly end up choosing their political parties based on the advertised policies that may appear more favourable to their immediate social or economical contexts rather than considering a wider holistic views on matters that are relevant to humanity at large.

For example, if you are a single struggling young mother, policies such as an increase in child benefits by a given political party might really appeal to you and you may end up voting for that party. On the other hand, someone else with no children, and worried about social spending may chose the opposite party. This is why our current governments, with very little accountability to their citizens, often get away with murder. Due to their narrow political ideologies, the ruling governments just please some sections of society at the expense of others. This is where the concept of a Global Human Assembly becomes attractive as it creates a united voice for all humanity and their demands from their governments. Since the governments are our servants, we need to fairly but intelligently keep them on a short leash and manage them carefully.

People selected in the assembly will become the representative owners of planet Earth and their requirements will be delivered through the government's actions. The Global Human Assembly will be bound by the same rules defined under the Human Principles.

This assembly cannot be another form of pseudo government with powers and perks. They will purely exist to keep the governments on track as the organised providers of services to our civilisation.

Amongst many sponsored intelligent social initiatives, the Global Human Assembly will be in charge of implementing the following:

- **Arms Eradication:** – We can never call ourselves civilised when we promote weapons and go to war. Therefore, globally we need to dismantle and eliminate the Arms industry in its entirety. Arms manufacturing, sales and the use of any lethal weapon will be made illegal. No individuals or groups including governments will ever be allowed to use barbaric arms to hurt, kill or destroy properties. The use of Arms by anyone will be regarded as a crime against humanity and will automatically carry serious consequences (to be defined by the Global Human Assembly).

- **Eradication of Human Cruelty:** – Total eradication of human cruelty across every corner and pocket of our planet is a major responsibility for the new social movement. There would be no excuse for people to systemically suffer through intentional actions of an individual, group or governments.

- Abolition of the flawed Market Economy: – This system has major endemic issues primarily based on slavery and feudalism. The existing Market Economy and its artificial monetary system are definitely not designed to serve humanity at large as they deliberately reward a few by systemically alienating and abusing many others. The type of social system we will need going forward is a one that can serve us and will be made to feed and prosper everyone. There are a number of alternative systems for our new social movement to adopt, such as the pioneering social systems that focus on social values as the measure rather than economic indicators.

A basic principle of modern state capitalism is that costs and risks are socialized to the extent possible, while profit is privatized.

—Noam Chomsky

- **End social competition & Promote Human Collaboration:** – The elimination of the concept of competition as a way of climbing the success ladder within our social context such as our communities, organisations and governmental establishment should be totally discouraged. The idea of competition, as previously explained, was purely based on the survival of the fittest and has the potential to cause major social diseases and disharmony. Our new society should be based on human collaboration towards achieving common goals and the prosperity of all.

- **Encourage Expression of Creativity:** – Our future society must remove any unnecessary preoccupation with our day to day survival needs. This should be through its application of intelligent and scientific means. By alleviating insecurities about our survival needs, humanity begins to feel at peace with the survival drivers and begins to freely explore available opportunities and contribute to others through encouraged creative pursuits.

- **Provision of Free Education:** – Every human being on earth has the right to free and quality education by the social system. Education is the most important means for human liberation and social advancement. It creates new ways of perceiving the world, thinking and helping humanity to sustainably coexist.

- **Provision of Free Food:** – Our new social system must ensure that every human being receives free quality food and beneficial nourishment. How can anybody watch others starving while they have plenty to eat? Such standards are far away from a healthy society.

- **Provision of Free Housing:** – As a civilised race we must recognise the primary human need for shelter. We need to ensure every human being can enjoy a safe and secure place to call home. Unless we can establish this, we run the risk of continuing to prolong human agony, creating an unstable and insecure world where people can panic and become unnecessarily preoccupied with their unpredictable social existence. This does not help our social cause or provide a cohesive society for us to live in.

- **Provision of Free Health:** – Statistically it is proven that through better health care services and better access to appropriate medicine/dietary regimes, rich people live much longer than poor people. As a civilised race we cannot allow such imbalances to unfairly continue to destabilise and divide our society to destruction.

In case you are wondering how we can globally provide free food, shelter and health to the people of the world, please read the pioneering scientific concepts presented by Jacque Fresco's in Venus project as just one example how things can be done. You must realise that people can easily be united to share, care and openly prosper through a holistic educational system and advance scientific methods that are already available to us right now. Please remember our sciences are so advanced at present that we can almost do anything we can imagine and there are absolutely no excuses for any of us to live barbarically in our staged world of chaos.

It is also incredibly immoral of our international governing bodies to conveniently ignore and dismiss potential civilised social solutions. Note that Jacque Fresco's work goes back to decades ago. Governments globally never paid any attention to such great social propositions, never explored or discussed such possibilities with their citizens.

Creation of the Global Scientific Assembly

This assembly will be the key body for the facilitation of practical scientific solutions for achieving our dream civilised social reform. The holistic application of the combined scientific disciplines can indeed finally eliminate our current global issues with food, shelter and health. It can truly allow people, plants, animals and the environment to prosper in harmony and sustained ways.

Although this group has total scientific independence for its discoveries, evaluation of issues and the application of holistic solutions to emerging social agendas, they are totally answerable and accountable to the Global Human Assembly for their achievements. Their performance is closely measured by how their bottom line contributions are serving humanity in accordance with rules stated by the Global Human Principles. On behalf of the Global Human Assembly, the Science Assembly will be setting standards, developing strategies and directly manging how governments operate and deliver parcels of social value.

This body should create innovative solutions for

how humanity can peacefully and harmoniously coexist. This group will overcome global challenges relating to our current lack of capabilities for the production and distribution of essential human needs such as food, shelter, health and education.

The Global Human Assembly will look to this group for holistic social solutions and ways of managing our Governments by socially measuring their performance and keeping them totally accountable.

In close working collaboration with the Global Social and Artistic Assembly (defined below), the Science Assembly will become responsible for the global educational management of humanity such as Pre- schools, schools and universities. The new educational system will have to be based on the true understanding of human needs and potential. Most importantly our education system will have to find effective ways to inspire and motivate humanity to openly learn, question and change the world for better.

The education delivered in our new social paradigm must be holistic in nature. It should include sciences, arts, but importantly, it must primarily be about understanding human nature and how we can harmoniously coexist with our dynamic ecosystem.

You can imagine a group of highly evolved individuals and knowledgeable scientists sitting harmoniously together to look at our social and environmental challenges. Each brings his or her own individual discipline and consideration forward to open-mindedly investigate the presenting issues from different dimensions and perspectives. They can make intelligent decisions based on causal relationships between all influencing factors to ensure the final solutions are the best possible options that can be made. The factors to be included in any social decision making process should carefully consider:

- Global Human Principles (the corner stone of humanity)
- Human needs (both physical, psychological and social)
- Environmental needs & influences (animal, plants and natural resources)

Creation of the Global Social and Artistic Assembly

This assembly will be the key body for the facilitation of practical social solutions and ensuing human needs are carefully considered and delivered. This Assembly will be closely working with the Scientific Assembly to ensure that our social issues are addressed from human, social and scientific dimensions. This body directly reports to the Global Human Assembly which is ultimately responsible for all our global social affairs.

The main Role of this assembly is to establish consensus amongst humanity: what human needs are and dictate the terms of how they may be satisfied by our available scientific know-how and the way our governments can deliver them. This Assembly will be directly responsible for managing the process of defining the Global Human Principles, establishing and maintaining an appropriate network of social and artistic representatives around the globe.

The focus of this assembly is also about how to enable human creativity and artistic talents to serve the society by setting appropriate parameters on how we may manage our new social structure. This body, through its extensive global networks, becomes the eyes, ears and voices of people around the world. It collects and assesses what is appropriate for humanity and how and when they should be met by the relevant governments.

Basic human needs based on the simple concept of Maslow hierarchy must be the main driver for our Social and Artistic Assembly. This includes basic human survival needs & safety, a sense of belonging, and the ability to positively contribute. It also has to ensure appropriate provisions for the creative manifestation of human inner potential.

Artistic freedom is about our expression of who we feel we are and how we wish to manifest our inner callings. It ties nicely to our core human need to self-express and freely contribute to the world.

The Future Role of our Governing Bodies

For humanity to be able to create its new nurturing social world, individuals must change and elevate their sense of self. They need to live a conscious existence and empower their personal will to be the main driver of their minds and allow them to truly believe that they deserve to have a good life as they are always unconditionally worthy. This means that we can spontaneously choose to experience a real sense of presence within our beings, feel beautiful and free of any imposed social limitations. We should collectively understand that if we can create our own realities through our deliberate intentions and projections of what we believe in, then we can let our powers create communities and governing bodies that can be especially designed to effectively serve us all. If every physical structure we see around us is made by people, then let's change and create new structures that can holistically serve us as deserving human beings.

Let us collectively manifest the emergence of a beautiful society. The main purpose behind the formation of any social structure is the creation of essential capabilities to serve humanity and nothing else. After all, we deliberately choose to join civilisations because the social benefits generated by some of their members can provide better lives for all of its population (a village hunting mentality to feed the whole village and not just a few), otherwise we might as well battle it out there alone.

We must take centre stage and realise the government of the day is purely elected by us to serve us as a <u>trusted servant</u>. Therefore governments of the future should be viewed as only a service provider to the big Boss – Humanity. We must mentally rise and recognise who is answering to whom in this society and bring proper measures of how things should be done in a civilised society. Have a say. We cannot limit ourselves by what social system we currently have, we need to question and change the system to serve us better and more effectively. We need to create new intelligent social structures that are vastly different from what we currently have.

In view of the past failed legacies of our governing bodies which are generally riddled with an inexcusable series of glaring shortfalls and mismanagement, please <u>don't ever</u> rely on your government's current intentions or capabilities to deliver future substance to humanity. For a real and effective solution, we need to think big and imagine well beyond our current political and limiting social frameworks. We need to see ourselves differently and reinvent ourselves differently as a global race.

For example, the overall concept of our protected borders and the separation of human clusters in our current global notion of nationhood will eventually have to disappear. Of course people will always be entitled to maintain and enjoy their local social/community heritage and ancestral ways or practices. However the concept of maintaining nationhood will no longer be intelligently or humanely viable in our newly designed concept of the global community.

In the future phases of our social evolution, there should be no more political cover ups labelled as the state secrets. By treating certain information as secret, today's governments inexcusably treat their average citizens either as simple minded fools, unworthy of being informed or they assumed people to be dangerous outsiders with subversive or risky potential. Therefore, in the government's mind, it is perfectly justified to keep them in the dark. Bit by bit they also take away our human rights and entitlement for privacy by creating staged adversaries and social fears. The public will never know what is real anymore.

In order to enjoy a great social future, we ideally need to establish a new political foundation that by design can attract and allow great holistic thinkers such as innovative social designers, well rounded scientists and humanitarian leaders to collaboratively be at the political helm of our new governing bodies. The existence of such an intelligent force will effectively result in balanced management and delivery of our civilised social needs. Their management will be about inspirational drive for successful manifestation of workable and sustainable social solutions.

> There will be no end to the troubles of states, or of humanity itself, till philosophers become kings in this world, or till those we now call kings and rulers really and truly become philosophers, and political power and philosophy thus come into the same hands.
>
> **—Plato**

People who can finally change this world for the better are definitely NOT the current simple minded politicians entrenched in their arcane political ideologies, but those from the stock of highly intelligent and holistic thinkers who have a real vision for creating a better civilised world. Our new social framework must seriously promote wider scope for perception, causal analysis of issues and proper decision making rigors based on solid facts and holistic sciences.

The establishment of such a modern political system has to occur organically in order to minimise social change impact and allow necessary time for governments to readjust and reinvent themselves. Before any good can come out of our governing bodies, first they have to fundamentally realign themselves and acquire necessary social and scientific intelligence and capabilities. This level of maturity will naturally take time, will require great determination to push through and explore the pure collaborative human spirit in action.

Gradually there will be an immense need for a formation of a World Government that will be directly responsible and answerable to the Global Human Assembly for meeting global human, social and environmental needs.

The transition from our current international paradigm that supports a multitude of independent sovereign governments to the notion of a single world government, may take some time, but such transition will be inevitable as our local social issues will not be effectively resolved unless we consider solutions from overall global perspectives (wider systemic approach to problem solving). In any case, our world is slowly becoming more homogeneous in terms of its diverse mix of people (for example, Australia's multicultural composition) that the concept of a world without borders is an inevitable future reality.

The danger we need to watch for is that the context in which the idea of a new World Government is meant to operate should not be mistaken or hijacked by the Self-Serving class concept of the World Order. We need to ensure the future World Government does not become a vehicle to enslave people, but to become totally answerable to people globally. It is also important to note that failed and toothless global institutions such as the United Nation will be totally irrelevant in such a future and will be no match for the proposed concept of the Global Human Assembly that actually represents the people's power on how they wish to drive governments as their elected servants rather than their rulers.

Phase-1 Constitutional Changes

In the initial phase we need to allow our current governments to continue managing their national affairs subject to a specific caveat that they will be fully responsible and accountable to the Global Human Assembly representative body established within individual countries. To achieve this we must find ingenious ways for changing the existing national constitutions within each sovereign state.

> The basis of our political system is the right
> of the people to make and to alter their
> constitutions of government.
> **—George Washington**

This is the first big hurdle for the Human Assembly to cross. It is expected that most governments will be totally reluctant or will not be given permission by their masters, the Self-Serving class, to allow ordinary people tamper with their arcane governing constitutions (our lame and unworkable system). This problem can only be overcome when the Global Human Assembly reaches a certain level of maturity and begins to represent a credible social force through its growing membership and by reaching the necessary critical mass. The mass organised movements can challenge the governments of the day head on and leave them no choice but to give in to the people' s power for change. The people's power to exercise their electoral rights can also contribute favourably to this dynamic for change.

> The most common way people give up their
> power is by thinking they don't have any.
> **—Alice Walker**

Phase-2 Governments Reshaping Themselves to Deliver Value

Once a sovereign government becomes more accountable as the deliverer of social needs and agendas, then

Human Assembly can gradually expect them to progressively embrace more and more of their national and international obligations and fine tune their machineries to deliver great social values.

Governments will be closely measured for every step they take and how effectively and holistically they continue to deliver parcels of human value. At this phase more and more governments are expected to safeguard the following:

- All political, social and scientific ideologies are to exist ONLY to holistically and sustainably serve humanity at large and all potential implementations have to be FULLY in line with the new globally agreed set of Human Principles.

- All decisions made within the governmental, social and business forums must totally include and ensure that Human Principles are honoured and under no circumstances are violated.

- The effective provision and distribution of essential materials and services to all people within national boundaries and within the context of global obligations are successfully met.

Phase-3 Birth of a World Government

Once the governments representing the sovereign countries begin to recreate themselves to deliver real substance in line with their national social expectations, the old global evils such as poverty, inequitable wealth distribution and lack of provision for essential social needs will begin to disappear. This in itself will be a massive improvement in terms of the overall health and fairness of our global social structure. Such improvements will directly result in more global social cohesion, gradual elimination of wars and conflicts that are generally fuelled by inequalities and lack of human rights. The World Government will naturally evolve as each social pocket of the world becomes more and more homogenously civilised in their overall conduct and the emergent humanitarian standards. It becomes purely a logical consideration for our governing bodies on how to effectively reorganise themselves and their diverse resources in order to deal with their global challenges more successfully.

15.

The Final Chapter

To summarise our human potential for social change and the creation of a better world for future generations to come, we must honestly and earnestly set out to explore all possibilities. In this chapter I summarise what I believe are appropriate and worthy points for individual and social consideration.

Let's start all over again and question everything we have with fresher eyes. What do we know with certainty about all those things we come into contact in this life? Let's itemise all the things we know to be true about what we intelligently observe around us. Following this understanding let's see how we can use logic and common sense as our building blocks and help manifest a wisely structured foundation for our coexistence and prosperity in life.

What do we know for a fact about the concept of self?

- **Accident of Birth & Death** – Without any prior awareness, we suddenly find ourselves in this world. Everything around us appears as a brand new experience or encounter. We build up concepts and become stronger as we go along and grow in life. We are logically aware that every living being eventually dies or appears to die. We superficially acknowledge the concept of death, but we have no understanding of what it actually means and we often find ourselves scared of encountering it.

- **Physical presence** – We often relate to ourselves within the limitation of our bodies. The body which we possess allows the 'I' to operate and do things in life. As our arms serve us to make things and create physical objects and our legs give us the mobility to geographically roam around. We interact with our world through physical, verbal and energetic means.

- **The 'I'** – We generally don't know what that sense of 'I' is and often see ourselves only as our bodies and for that reason we just live to serve and maintain our body's needs, and sometimes to unreasonable extremes.

- **Sense of Purpose** – From the systemic perspective, every object and being exists to serve a unique purpose in life. This means that this 'I' is here to achieve something valuable and this 'I' is not here just to indulge the body with luxuries. Sadly the importance of our sense of purpose in life is hardly ever discussed in social forums or openly regarded as the <u>only reason we are born in this world</u>.

- **Programed for Survival** – The body has physical and psychological needs in order to remain healthy and functioning. We are primarily driven to meet our survival needs and reduce daily choirs through creative human qualities that can automate what appears to us as burdensome.

- **Crave social peace** – We look for opportunities to meet our physical and psychological needs in life. We are naturally programmed to gravitate to the notion of home and family. It feels very natural to feel secure within the confinement of home with mum, dad and siblings somewhere in the background. It is within our genes to belong and feel safe and protected. This is exactly what we all want from life and expect from our social leaders (to belong, feel safe and protected). The concept of community is a very natural human concept for wanting to belong, learn and grow in a safe environment. Therefore it seems we already have a great theme to build upon. That is in order to maintain a civilised state of existence, people simply expect their basic needs to be equitably met and realise there are sustainable social possibilities for them to holistically prosper.

- **Sense of Contribution & Worthiness** – We all want to have impressive output and feel worthy in terms of how capable we are in contributing to the wider world, make our mark and be noticed. When our contribution is aligned with our sense of purpose, we thrive and enjoy our lives with great sense of satisfaction.

- **Creative by nature** – We are truly creative by nature and the deepest joy we experience in life is when we do something well and make it public to make a difference.

- **Sense of despair** – When events become overwhelming and we consciously find it hard to cope with stress. Of course stress is our best friend that tells us we are not doing the right thing in our lives through our existing internal beliefs and behaviour. That is when we become slaves to habits and unworkable beliefs.

What do we know for a fact about our outer world?

We need to question what sort of world we are actually living in and how we are impacted by myriads of life forces and experiences. Learn to understand and listen to nature through available sciences, metaphysical perspectives and artistic forms. Once we understand what naturally governs us in life and how we can establish which relationship with these forces are constantly shaping our collective moments and shared experiences in life, we genuinely qualify to help change our current world for the better.

We can't change or manifest anything unless we know what we want and how life can change from that point on for us and others impacted by our intentions.

So we need to understand our environment and its rules. It is not that hard.

The hologram – There is a dreamy feel about life and how we experience events around us. Before we begin to manifest our own version of reality and change our world, we should realise that we live within the context of a hologram and for this, we have to learn how the hologram works and the kind of rules we are governed by.

The reason we may think life has holographic qualities is due to how our human senses sit between the concept of self (the 'I') and what we imagine the world out there to be. Our senses project in our heads a version of what reality may be out there, but we never really know what is actually out there. For this reason everything that we observe with our senses could be regarded as a hologram of what is projected as real, but not necessarily the reality itself.

The simplest way to change our hologram is by starting to chip away and change the smallest fragments within our total life structure and once that is accomplished, the rest of the structure will simply tumble, change and create the desired picture of our reality as we expect it. So in life by changing the smallest aspect of our day to day conduct, we literally set in motion internal precedence for changing our entire self in due course. You sow the seed and the change will take place organically over time.

Since the life hologram governs us 24x7, by understanding its rules and seeing them as our best potential for greater intelligence, we can manifest far more effectively and shape our world as we please.

Micro & macro – Without exception, every object in this world is part of a larger structure and it is also made up of much smaller divisible parts. This concept repeats itself endlessly at both the macro and micro levels. Such consistent fractal qualities in how life is structured assist us in our greater understanding and management of things we can't see and easily measure. For example, we can't visibly observe the entire universe or microscopically view atoms; however, we can deduce important understanding about their qualities and potential through what we can easily see and measure in our immediate surroundings.

Influences of the birth place – It is true that every human being has a unique and almost predestined base to begin with. Why do we have the life we have and not someone else's? For example, why am I born in UK and you are born in a small village in Africa? Why do I have more obvious privileges in life than you who through no choice of your own ended up living in a small village deprived of basic amenities? This represents a bigger question for us that the total picture is not just about us manifesting realities, but it is also about what our physical and social settings are (our starting point in life). Through no conscious fault of our own, we can have pleasant or unpleasant starting life foundations. This is within a mix of the physical, social and political environment that we are born to. For example, it is much harder to rise and shine as a star out of an African ghetto than it is from a wealthy and established social position in life.

Is there an accident of birth or is there no accident and if so what does it mean? Why is it that our individual souls on their arrival on earth encounter different and sometimes contrasting ways and experiences? Why can't we all begin life with the same opportunities? Why are we treated unequally by life itself? Why is there such massive disparity in terms of the level of opportunities we can receive in a favourable birth environment verses any difficult and malnourished environment we may encounter?

It is a given that individuals at the time of birth bring to this life their unique set of personality traits that clearly differentiate them from one another. For those who believe in the concept of reincarnation, the individual traits may be explained by the qualities they bring with themselves from their past life existences.

As a clinical hypnotherapist practicing over many years, I have come across many bizarre cases where without any plausible explanation, some individuals revert back to experiences from their past lives and somehow they begin to access information that logically cannot make any sense to us. People can accurately describe places they have never been before and sometimes they label them as Deja vu. Refer to work by Brian Weiss – MD.

For example, I know of a case which was well

documented by a hypnotherapist where an individual under hypnosis accurately described a box buried under the floor board of a house in a country that this individual had never visited in this life time. There are other well documented cases where people under hypnosis somehow unexplainably begin to fluently speak a foreign language that they consciously know nothing about. Of course such convincing evidence by itself does not provide sufficient proof for the existence of past life, but at the minimum, these cases explain that we have potential access to information well beyond our apparent physical existence on earth.

Although I can't categorically explain why the accident of birth may exist, it is plausible to assume that if we accept the premise that we potentially bring our past identity and mind-set into this life for further refinement or resolution, it also makes sense that we need to be born in a specific or required environment in order for us to address those initial personality charges that were not resolved in our past lives.

The Cyclical Law of Opposites – Nothing lasts forever in this amazing mystery called life. All social events of great significance somehow just spring into existence when the environment is conducive for them to flourish, socially impact us for a while and eventually totally disappear out of existence as if they never existed. It appears there is a cyclical pattern in how life fluctuates over time and allows opposite forces to take turns to manifest into state of existence and finally disappear as they give way to their rivals to take over. So on that basis, we need to value every event in life as a great teacher and let each encounter cognitively evolve and prepare us for the next set of experiences to come. For this reason we should never get either too arrogant about our current favourable positions or worse, feel drowned in sorrows for difficult experiences we may encounter in life. Remember, it is cyclical and at each complete turn, we developmentally ascend just a little bit higher than the last time.

We can intelligently perceive and assess what life dishes out to us as an intended blessing for our next life stage development, even though on the surface, events may appear to be adversarial and force us to deal with unexpected challenges. We should refuse to look back at them and view them with regret or trepidation, but only perceive them as life mysteries intended to provide us the necessary evolutionary jolts and new opportunities for our personal growth. Out of every scenario, we must always look for lessons that can potentially influence us to holistically and wisely do better things next time around. That is the evolutionary path to our deeper desires for knowing our true self (our soul). Each time we go through a full life cycle of contrasting experiences, we begin again repeating similar life experiences, but each time, with a new set of opportunities and greater wisdom than last time around. You may think of it as our ascension through a spiral growth of self-knowing.

Conscious Manifestation of Reality – Based on our recent scientific discoveries about our human potential that we have innate capabilities to project and manifest our own reality through what we believe is possible, we should feel privileged and empowered with our new life prospects. This is really encouraging for humanity to realise that at last we can imagine our intentions and guide them towards their final state of manifested reality and achieving them purely through believing that everything in life is possible.

The concept of self-projection and manifestation of desires into physical realities are quite appealing to many of us who seek possibilities for better lives. So now we know since we have been reassured by our scientific communities that we have the required capabilities to create better outcomes in our lives if we choose to do so.

The sobering narratives used in explaining our current state of social demise in this book may appear seriously shocking to some readers, but unfortunately we must face them all and wisely learn from them. Unless the truth is told about who we are and what our rights are as a deserving race of civilised human beings, there is no escape for the innocents from their continuing world of oppression, blindfolded slavery and undignified human treatment under the political disguise of good social governance.

In my view enough is enough of deliberate human mismanagement. Where is our intelligence and why do we feel so helpless that we can't logically establish a civilised social reality and peace for ourselves? What is wrong with us and why can't we just do it and take charge of our social affairs?

The simple historical answer is that we always have had all the required ability and the necessary intelligence to do anything we want and much more, but what has stopped us up to now is our sense of despair and the way we often belittle ourselves that we are helpless and not in any position to win against the presented odds. At times, we may feel the loss of not having the necessary wisdom to help us rally sufficient transformative capabilities to successfully indent, crack or fundamentally reshape our current uncivilised ways and remove our grimy social foundations. But now we know that we can project our intentions forward and overcome both our futile sense of despair and the feelings that we are incapable to act.

Following what has been expressed in this book and your wider exposure to 'what is' and 'what is possible' in our world, now we have real options to choose from.

We can calmly rise above the initial shocks, overcome our sense of despair about our current social horrors and see these events not only just as unpleasant episodes in our lives, but view them as a transient state of our human evolutionary journey.

We can interpret this social journey as the necessary stepping stones toward achieving a greater future social reform. We can consciously choose to feel more inspired or even privileged that we can intelligently make a lasting difference to our lives, leave a legacy and intentionally progress forward on our peaceful and collective journey of global social reform.

Self-healing tips

Let us raise our imaginary mental anchors and together set sail into civilised ways of being and enjoy our peaceful lives as a blessed race of humanity. But remember first and foremost, we need to heal the self before we make any attempt to change or heal our current social structure. In order to heal the self from the tarnishes of our social conditioning, one must begin to truly understand the self, recognise its needs and rights. Then willingly self-expand to see others as the extension of self, which will begin to reach out to others with love and compassion. We can see the self as a much larger expanse of physical self that is constantly trying to merge to the ultimate truth & possibilities. You can feel that you are integrally connected to everything and everyone. Mental and physical borders or boundaries will disappear. Barriers can no longer hold together as we feel mentally free from social biases and fears. We can literally dance with joy rather than miserably and unintelligently cry.

Waking up – Unfortunately as the majority of people are literally sleep walking, they unconsciously reinforce their own social conditioning and daily sorrows, especially when they unashamedly become creatures of habits in their lives (predictable). Basically that is when we become less and less interested in looking for new solutions to our needs as we unconsciously close doors to life opportunities by purely resisting change and feed on our daily chemical addictions for our daily dose of misery.

G.I. Gurdjieff believed that the majority of people in this world are simply sleepwalking and hardly ever consciously operating (robot like state). So our daily awakening from the robotic state should be the foremost disciplined practise. Otherwise our conscious mind relentlessly becomes tricked by the power and influences of our subconscious beliefs.

Through the internal chemical changes and strange voices we often hear in our ears, our destiny becomes sealed in concrete as we feel compelled to follow our unconscious demands on how we should react to life encounters. We can experiment by consciously calling the subconscious's habitual bluffs; resisting its commands and observing how much 'conscious will' we actually have at our disposal.

This is what Gurdjieff elegantly referred to as '<u>Intentional sufferings & Conscious Labour</u>'. Basically if you can consciously override what you are deeply feeling, you literally take charge of your conscious destiny and little by little free yourself from your prior social conditionings.

Encouraging our Intuitions – The human heart is the seat of our consciousness's awareness. I believe the 'I's' intelligence is the heart's intelligence, pure and untarnished by the biases of our subconscious beliefs. Of course, our heart does not think or chatter as it just unbiasedly and instinctively views the world as is. On the other hand, based on its dedicated robotic nature, the mind uses its beliefs and conditioning to think, make decisions in order to keep the body alive and meet human survivals needs. However as we have already explained in detail, if we allow our minds to freely dictate and run us without any checks and balances, we (the real 'I' within us) become the second class citizen in our own kingdom as the servant will become elevated to run the entire show(our lives).

According to a number of researches conducted over the past two decades by various groups around the world such as the work by Dr Rollin McCraty and Dr Raymond Trevor Bradley, the heart receives information before our brain does and that heart is an information processing center that can learn, remember, and act independently of the cranial brain. It is understood that the heart actually connects and sends signals to key brain areas such as the amygdala, thalamus, and hypothalamus, which regulate our perceptions and emotions. It seems we have a second "brain" in our chest.

Promotion of Self-Love – Love yourself unconditionally. Why? Simply because you exist. The body and the mind are part of the overall package you unconsciously brought into this life. Therefore accept the total package, but always make sure you train it well with whatever you have, heal it from old and constrictive beliefs and live as a liberated soul searching individual. Always be proud of yourself for being here on this planet. How lucky is that to simply experience life. Think of the alternative – no experiences what so ever. No hint of what existence actually is. How deprived it seems.

Remember self-love is about **self-kindness, self-acceptance** and **self-forgiveness**. So if we are kind to ourselves we should always refuse to become tricked by our internally generated negative emotions that forcefully encourage us to feel miserable and continue to make us live as hypnotised stressed individuals. All because our uncontrolled emotions ultimately win every time, rule us and tell us how we should actually feel in accordance with previous experiences of hurts and social conditionings.

So recognise how our negative emotional charges can deplete our overall vital energies to no avail. Therefore consciously intervene by refusing to live in fear, feel guilty for anything or allow anger to rule your life on a permanent basis. Remember our emotions should only serve us as a barometer. Their impact should only be felt momentarily as a reminder of how we view things internally and they should never become permanent features in our lives as they would literally destroy us mentally and physically.

For example, if you consciously desire to be happy rather than sad in life, then from that point on consciously choose to command your mind to never allow any of your internal beliefs and their generated emotions to make you feel sad. Just use your will to override your emotions and stay consciously in charge of your happiness. If you can't achieve that, then you would instinctively know that your emotions are driving your decisions and action, rather than your objective assessment of the situation (call it intelligence).

Intelligently Seek Quality of life – Unless we stop and genuinely question what matters most to us and consciously seek those qualities that can bring us true satisfaction in life, we could end up following someone else's dream or aspirations.

The way we may achieve our quality of life is first by understanding our sense of purpose (what deeply pleases us to achieve what is outside our usual daily self-pampering). As stated earlier, we are not here just to look after and indulge our bodies. By only following such pursuits we may please our bodies by providing them with many material possessions and physical comforts, but by purely focusing on self, we unconsciously defy the main reason why we are born – That is 'to effectively and creatively do things to please our souls such as willingly contributing to our wider world.

In spite of having many life comforts and social successes, those who only live to self-promote and self-serve, at some point will undoubtedly wake up and experience an unexplainable sense of emptiness. Of course it is essential for us to look after ourselves holistically and there is nothing wrong with physical comfort per se, however, we maintain our bodies so they can actually perform something special for us – 'meet our sense of purpose in life'.

To understand our sense of purpose, we simply need to understand what we creatively and willingly enjoy doing in life and that is the vehicle for satisfying our sense of purpose. If I love playing music, then perhaps I can contribute to my world through my music or if I enjoy exploring scientific concepts, perhaps I can help the world through such passions. It does not have to be something big, but it has to be satisfying. You could perhaps hold someone's hand and help them with their basic needs and if this brings satisfaction to your life, then that may be your purpose. Many parents do just that by working hard to raise healthy and happy children. I believe we are very capable of doing many creative and wonderful things to satisfy our need, to reach out and make a difference.

Holistically Nurture the Body – Since the body is the 'I''s body suit, the appropriate nurturing of our bodies is highly essential and it is the extension of the concept of self-love that goes some way in honouring our devoted servant (the body). Our body should be looked after similar to the way we look after our cars or any useful devices that we are totally dependent on and would be lost without them. For this, we need to eat healthy food, exercise and rest adequately. But most importantly we should not take out life's frustrations on our bodies either by physically damaging it or letting our negative emotions make our bodies sick.

Daily Meditation Practices – On a daily basis, every physical or mental move we make naturally causes stress in our bodies. Our Sympathetic Nervous System is designed to make us stressed and it kicks in to help us stretch ourselves to do what is necessary in our daily activities. As we finally rest, our Parasympathetic Nervous System then becomes active and repairs the damage caused by our earlier stress. This amazing complementary natural process allows us to stay in balance on a daily basis. However, if we are stressing more than resting or recuperating, our Parasympathetic Nervous System become less and less effective in repairing and creating the necessary balance in our bodies. For this reason we can progressively become more and more stressed to the point that our Parasympathetic Nervous System forgets how to help us out of our dire situation. The only way to help remedy this is through a conscious practice of meditation and self-hypnosis. The continuous daily meditation allows us to teach our bodies to rest and restore the ability of our Parasympathetic Nervous System to work effectively.

In view of our imposed and unregulated social pressures, the majority of human beings around the world find it more and more difficult to have a healthy work life balance. The statistics are alarming how we are losing the battle against our stressful life style and physically and mentally becoming sicker as a race. So instead of resorting to quick fixes such as drowning ourselves in drugs or alcohol in order to alleviate and numb our senses, we can learn to meditate, rise above our stress and create mental clarity in how to save ourselves and change our chaotic world.

As a great advocator of meditation, I can't say enough about the therapeutic value of what it brings to our lives. In my clinical practice, I openly promote the benefits meditation brings to our lives and how it can balance us mentally and physically. I often say to my clients that the practice of meditation is just as important if not more important than their daily food intake.

The other powerful aspect of meditation is that it also allows us to visualise ourselves not just in our physical sense of 'I', but also in the way it builds connections with the real essence of self (the 'I'). It makes us realise our integral connection with everyone and everything we come to contact with. It also allows us to become more conscious in the way we perceive the bigger picture and think and act towards others.

Social healing tips

In my view what really gives us the strength to embark, influence and change our world the way we desire is that there are no impossible barriers that can stop us as a race to achieve anything we want to achieve. Collectively we have every single capability that is required.

If we are feeling free mentally, then without question our larger world will also be free. The following tips are aimed at focusing on the most essential theme that we can adopt in our journey towards social reform.

Decipher the Truth from the Myth – We always need to be open to what we observe, but use our intelligence and objectivity before accepting what is proposed as reality. This means we need to put our emotions aside and almost scientifically look at the presented facts. In my view, it is more intelligent and beneficial in the long term to embrace a painful truth than to live in joyful lies.

Since we are constantly bombarded, or at times drowned by our official and social media, we need to train our minds to differentiate wisely between real information and misinformation which are often hard to set apart. Otherwise we can have misinformed views of unfolding events in our world and become deceived or conditioned by those who wish to manipulate us.

Understand Life Causal Forces – Learn from the micro and macro perspectives in life. Understand how objects and forces around us interrelate with one another. This is crucial for when we are analysing and adjusting our environment for the better. Understand how our actions can both directly and indirectly impact our environment and for this, why we must minimise any potential damage and do no harm when applying solutions to problems at hand. Far too often social decisions are made in silos and in the absence of wider human and environmental contexts.

If you look at everything that has ever gone wrong in our society, you soon notice it is because people never comprehended the true nature of their emerging situations and they either ignorantly or maliciously ignored holistically assessing the dynamics of the environment they were meant to be operating within and too often people acted hastily and without real understanding of the causal implication of their actions.

For example, every single war or conflict that the world has ever witnessed, without exception, falls in that broad category. Because if normal people knew upfront about the eventual consequences of what these wars could bring to their world, no matter how insistent their leaders may have been in favour of such atrocity, people would have intelligently and categorically refused to participate in them.

For example, in hindsight, people would have totally objected and never supported the inhumane and futile war in Iraq that created mayhem, destabilised the entire Middle East and allowed the barbaric ISIS to flourish under false pretexts and fabrication by the Self-Serving class.

So here is our chance to actively foresee what may happen with the existing political plans or impending proposals for yet another stupid 'war that we really must have' or the inexcusable apathy for taking the right steps against climate change. Before it is too late, think about the consequences of our current silo driven global mind-set and short-sighted political decisions.

Our basic intelligence tells us that we need to analyse much deeper and take holistic actions toward our challenges rather than prolonging or transferring our issues to another time or place.

Be Involved – We are born to interact with one another, grow and contribute to our social world. Since we are part of the systemic fabric of life, there is no way we can avoid the fact that social interactions and contributions are at the core essence of our beings.

Many of our social issues exist due to the fact that many people have been innocently conditioned to focus only on their immediate challenges and stay away from direct participations in their social and political affairs. We need to change such disempowering social behaviours and consciously feel responsible for all our social and political decisions and actions. Through such a collective voice and intent we can bring to order what we may regard as inhumane, cruel and unnecessary. We must not allow our social pressures (For example, 'to keep up with Joneses' or preoccupation with our daily survival) distract us and push us away from being involved in what truly matters in life (our social and political affairs).

So we need to become curious about what decisions are made in our names by those who are meant to serve us equitably and represent us honourably. If we wash our hands of such crucial social participation, we should no longer complain about our world of chaos and manipulation.

Since the majority of our past and current social failings rest with how our leaders have been mismanaging our social affairs, we who vote and bring such leaders into power must now become socially informed about what actually goes on around us and measure how politicians are performing. Therefore, we all have ethical duties to raise awareness, share around and educate others with what we know to be true and relevant in our social world. In my view, education is the most effective way for bringing social reform into successful manifestation. We must all become ambassadors for the truth and what constitutes as human rights. We must help those who are in the dark to become awakened.

Promote Human Unity and Avoid Divisions – Since we are all together in this space called life, we can't possibly avoid one another, create a divided society and yet prosper collectively. It is impossible. Based on the systemic principles that govern us, we are much stronger together and better off than individually pursuing success in isolation. Therefore to succeed as a race, we must find ways to unite together and collaboratively work through our issues.

We need to learn to communicate openly and unbiasedly see potential in opposing views and resolve differences intelligently so we can communally prosper.

The best way to avoid conflict is to collectively agree on fundamental and basic human values that unite and define who we are as a civilised human race. Once that is achieved, the rest is the question of 'how' we can effectively get there. In order to agree how to get there, we can use **logic** and evaluate all proposed methods in view of their holistic nature and contribution. A successful proposal will need to go through rigors how broadly it is aligned with the dynamics of our world of cause and effect. It will also be assessed by how effectively adopted solutions are honouring those initial human values we collectively agreed upon. After all, as human beings we have common social needs and on that basis there is a greater common ground between us than what differentiates us. Our differences are due to method of doing things the way we prefer rather than the differences in the substance they were meant to deliver.

Final Conclusion

In the introduction, I proposed an important question to my readers: why humanity has been so cruelly short-changed and forced to live in the current diabolical and compromised social structure. Even those who appear to be relatively better off are still highly impacted by waves of daily global social turmoil and the causal implication of the current injustices in our shrinking global world. Our world has become inescapably small, accessible and it is increasingly converging on itself and becoming highly interconnected.

As we progressed in the book, we clarified that the majority of the population of the world (99%) **does not want or like uncivilised existence**. The best way to validate this statement is by simply asking everybody you know in your life if they naturally gravitate towards inhumanity in preference to living in peace and harmony. Remember people do not start wars, governments do. This truth should have a significant resonance with those who are genuinely and intelligently seeking a workable solution for creating a better world. Because unless we understand what holds us back, wake up from our mass hypnotic state and recognise our forgotten powers, we can never excel to create a future dream world.

The root cause examination of our current undesirable social system revealed there are far more sinister and manipulative reasons that are almost unimaginable and hard to digest by ordinary people. In our findings we also clarified it is totally unintelligent for anyone to buy into the official explanation and the psychological suggestion that our so called animalistic human tendencies are the reason why the world is dysfunctional and barbaric. We discovered we are used as a scapegoat and blamed our <u>innate cruel and greedy human nature</u>, as the reason why we need to be forcefully manhandled; controlled and mismanaged by various violent institutions we call 'government of the day'.

As part of legitimising their manufactured lies that people are innately uncivilised, our official establishments openly endorse the use of force and unimaginable destructive weapons to beat sense into us and shape us into submissive or unquestioning citizens. They also senselessly advocate that they are doing it to protect humanity against itself ('us' should always beat the hell out of 'them' disregarding of the fact that both sides are just ordinary people and made of flesh and blood).

Through our journey, we also learnt that human beings are not by nature barbarians and as a matter of fact they are far more loving, caring, nurturing and collaborative than how they are inexcusably demonised and portrayed by a handful of influential barbarians currently ruling the world. If at times people act ignorantly, it is because they are socially conditioned to compete with one another, climb on top of each other, fear or hate one another. The smallest differences between people are often covertly exaggerated by the system to create a storm in a teacup. This is successfully achieved by the spread of misinformation, socially divisive suggestions and autosuggestions so people slowly begin to psychologically believe in the exaggerated differences. Their minds start to accept the gap between 'us' and 'them' is too big: that no compromise can be reached so they choose a side and are happy to fight for their false and manufactured beliefs.

We also discussed that those of us who may have been severely conditioned by social manipulators and believe in the official lies, are becoming less and less relevant to the intellectual debates that are currently sweeping the world with many awakened and questioning individuals. Have you notice how many new forums are born every day challenging existing social beliefs and paradigm. Governments can no longer dismiss or point fingers at those who question this unworkable and broken system. They have no right to label the questioning citizens as subversive, delusional or 'one of them'.

Even if some individuals refuse to believe in a wide spread world-wide conspiracy explanation, surely common sense alone should encourage them to re-evaluate their beliefs when they consider it is absolutely impossible for 1% of the population to easily acquire 95% of the global wealth without direct assistance from their official governing bodies. It is also impossible to achieve such unimaginable wealth without the assistance of a well organised clandestine mega machine to fuel its greedy existence. This happens unashamedly right in front of our eyes while the other 99% of the population are fundamentally deprived and missing out on what should legitimately be their share.

We were also astounded to learn that most governments conveniently forget to honour their commitments to their people. As regulators, governments all over the world conveniently fail to ensure an equitable distribution of wealth amongst their citizens. Surely the notion of 'governments are there to serve their citizens' must be the biggest and cruellest social joke of all times. The most intelligent question that everybody should be asking is <u>who is actually running the world</u> and why there is no visible accountability anywhere to be seen.

For example, if ordinary people commit the most basic crime, they could easily end up in jail with the full force of the law applied to them, but governments can somehow sponsor state terrorism (called 'War') on a mass scale and openly kill thousands of innocent people in clandestine wars and without any repercussion and totally get away with their openly executed genocides as if the rule of law somehow falls short for some sectors in our society. Just think about the thousands of innocent people that have died/ been murdered to no avail and became displaced in Afghanistan and Iraq <u>alone</u>, while Bush, Blair and Howard governments (the coalition of willing) have absolutely nothing to answer for or bow to anyone. I wonder how the victims' relatives feel about such visible and deliberate injustices.

We need to wonder why we can't have a say in our general wellbeing and our long term peaceful social prosperity. Why are we unnecessarily suffocating and brutally mismanaged as a race? Why are we denied the ability to excel and refused the opportunity to live joyfully in our entitled paradise called mother Earth?

Think of the possibility and the excitement of having all the required technology and intelligence to create a dream paradise of joy, learning and contribution to a meaningful life right here and now.

We were outraged to know that humanity has everything it needs right now to change the world into a paradise of love, beauty and peace for all to share and enjoy. The question is why are we hanging around and unnecessarily suffocating? Who is preventing us achieving our human rights and desire for a better social life? It appears the problem lies with us for not standing up for what truly matters to us, or follow through what we believe in. There is no body more powerful than us (ordinary people) to initiate and implement fundamental social change.

We also learnt that charity should always start from home and why it is important to first clean our inner mental citadel from negative clutter, biases, disempowering beliefs and prior psychological conditioning before committing ourselves to a wider social reform. The reason for this personal reform is that it gives us a chance as humanity to start again, see ourselves and others with a fresh and liberating set of perspectives and empowering beliefs that are vastly different to how we are socially conditioned and raised to be. There should be no 'us and them' anymore to create conflicts and divide humanity into dysfunctional silos of fear, hate and fractured human unity.

> Out beyond ideas of wrongdoing and rightdoing there is a field. I'll meet you there. When the soul lies down in that grass, the world is too full to talk about. Do you know what you are? You are a manuscript

of a divine letter. You are a mirror reflecting
a noble face. This universe is not outside of
you. Look inside yourself; everything that
you want, you are already that.

—Rumi

Our civilised social journey towards equitable prosperity is totally within our current human potential, given capabilities and grasp. However to get to that point so we can individually and collectively commit to some form of intelligent and peaceful movement for upholding our human rights, we first need to actively participate and let others hear about our personal views and human perspectives. Common sense tells us that **we need to uphold our human rights and values and build <u>our entire social structure</u> around them**.

We can take the first step in our liberating human journey by creating a Global Human Movement for the purpose of defining and elevating the power of ordinary people onto the political centre stage. The only method that can create a new Human Movement is through the propagation of real insights, delivery of meaningful education and raising human awareness through social media and organised events. We constantly need to seek facts and the real truth behind our conditioning and current unexplainable world tragedies.

Our first significant outcome will become possible through the collective act of defining and upholding the first **Global Human Principles** (<u>Global Human Bill of Rights</u>). This will become an instrument for holding all world governments accountable to honour such rights. In this scenario, governments will only exist to uphold such principles and they must regard the mandate as the reason they are currently employed – **to serve humanity caringly, equitably and sustainably by using the basic God given intelligence.**

This Bill of Rights is not defined by governments; it is defined by the actual people of the world and will explain precisely what type of delivery people expect from their serving governments. This Bill is a set of principles by which governments can continue to operate and are measured as **good servants** to humanity.

Therefore, we ALL have direct responsibility for the wellbeing of ourselves, others and our world at large. We must work together and embrace the notion of – **what is good for all must be good for one and what is good for one must be good for all.**

If people are truly united in thoughts and actions toward a great human cause, it is inevitable that success would magically eventuate simply through the sheer magnitude of the collective and focussed human spirit carrying with it the <u>human future destiny</u> in its own hands.

If we do not participate and become involved in the social decision making process that could causally impact and shape our future life, as a race we shall miss a golden opportunity to make a difference and claim our civilised rights to a peaceful global existence. If we do nothing, we seal our own destiny for choosing to continue to stay silent with 'business as usual' and permitting the same challenges to continue bothering us and making us bitter about life as we go forward.

<u>Make a difference and feel good that you truly have powers to manifest as you wish</u>

I Simply Matter to Myself and the World at Large

www.soltanitherapy.com.au